BY

JEANNE ROBERT FOSTER

[Julie Ollivier]

BOSTON
SHERMAN, FRENCH & COMPANY
1916

TO

J. B. YEATS, R.H.A.

WHEN I AM DEAD

When I am dead,—
Do I wish for beauty remembered for aye as a sun-bright gem
To coronal me through all the years with a deathless diadem?
Do I wish my name to be as a Master-Word,
Whispered wherever the awe and terror of power is stirred.
No, none of this,—
Neither beauty nor power,—for the groping hands of men
Will scatter my dust from its quiet place, and re-create me again.
No, only this,—
The sound of my singing voice, far-falling on alien seas,
Telling the strange, wild ways of the heart,—of life's full cup, and the lees,—
Heard at high noon
As a note that compassed the gamut of earth and sky,
That ran with the sweeping storm in the vault where the thunders die,—

Heard through the dawn,—
In the throat of the brown peewits and sparrows that build in the eaves,
In the hedge flower's bursting bud, and the trembling sound of the leaves.
Heard in the wind,—
With that unutterable sound of passionate breath,
The gasp of a quickened life when love goes down unto death.

CONTENTS

I THE GREAT SEA FIGHT AND OCCASIONAL POEMS

II SONNETS

III SONGS, BALLADS, PASTORALS

V SILHOUETTES

VI ORIFIEL

VII THE EVE OF SANHAIN

I

THE GREAT SEA FIGHT AND OCCASIONAL POEMS

1

THE GREAT SEA FIGHT

In my watch on deck at the turn of the night
  I saw the spindrift rise,
And I saw by the thin moon's waning light
  The sheen of dead men's eyes.
They rose from the wave in armor bright,
  The men who never knew fear;
They rose with their swords to their hips strapped tight,
  And stripped to their fighting gear.

I hauled below, but to and fro
  I saw the dead men glide,
With never a plank their bones to tow,
  As the slippery seas they ride.
While the bale-star burned where the mists swayed low
  They clasped each hand to hand,
And swore an oath by the winds that blow —
  They swore by the sea and land.

They swore to fight till the Judgment Day,
  Each night ere the cock should crow,
Where the thunders boom and the lightnings play
  In the wrack of the battle-glow.
They swore by Drake and Plymouth Bay,
  The men of the Good Hope's crew,
By the bones that lay in fierce Biscay;
  And they swore by Craddock, too —

That every night, ere the dawn flamed red,
  For each man there should be twain
Upon the ships that make their bed
  Where England rules the main.
They pledged — and the ghost of Nelson led —
  When the last ship's gunner fell
They would man the guns — these men long dead —
  And ram the charges well.

So we'll choose the night for the Great Sea Fight,
  Nor ever give chase by day;
Our compeers rise in the white moonlight,
  In the wash of the flying spray;
And if we fall in the battle-blight,
  The shade of a man long dead
Fights on till dawn on the sea burns bright
  And Victory, overhead!

THE *WILLIAM P. FRYE*

I SAW her first abreast the Boston Light
At anchor; she had just come in, turned head,
And sent her hawsers creaking, clattering down.
I was so near to where the hawse pipes fed
The cable out from her careening bow,
I moved up on the swell, shut steam and lay
Hove to in my old launch to look at her.
She'd come in light, a-skimming up the Bay
Like a white ghost with topsails bellying full;
And all her noble lines from bow to stern
Made music in the mind; it seemed she rode
The morning air like those thin clouds that turn
Into tall ships when sunrise lifts the clouds
From calm sea-courses.

There, in smoke-smudged coats,
Lay funneled liners, dirty fishing craft,
Blunt cargo-luggers, tugs and ferry boats.
Oh, it was good in that black-scuttled lot
To see the *Frye* come lording on her way
Like some old queen that we had half forgot
Come to her own. A little up the Bay
The Fort lay green, for it was springtime then;
The wind was fresh, rich with the spicy bloom
Of the New England coast that tardily
Escapes, late April, from an icy tomb.
The Statehouse glittered on old Beacon Hill,

Gold in the sun . . . 'Twas all so fair awhile;
But she was fairest — this great square-rigged ship
That had blown in from some far happy isle
Or from the shores of the Hesperides.

They caught her in a South Atlantic Road
Becalmed and found her hold brimmed up with wheat;
" Wheat's contraband," they said, and blew her hull
To pieces, murdered one of our stanch fleet,
Fast dwindling, of the big old sailing ships
That carried trade for us on the high sea
And warped out of each harbor in the States.
It wasn't law, so it seems strange to me —
A big mistake. Her keel's struck bottom now
And her four masts sunk fathoms, fathoms deep
To Davy Jones. The dank sea-weed will root
On her oozed decks, and the cross-surges sweep
Through the set sails; but never, never more
Her crew will stand away to brace and trim,
Nor sea-blown petrels meet her threshing up
To windward on the Gulf Stream's stormy rim;
Never again she'll head a no'theast gale
Or like a spirit loom up, sliding dumb,
And ride in safe beyond the Boston Light,
To make the harbor glad because she's come.

ROBERT LANIER

(*In memoriam*)

O YE Eternal Voices, say he could not die,—
This poet-soul, the youngest, best-beloved!
So brief his flight, so short his nesting time,
Hardly within him had ripe genius moved;
No thought of self had ever warped his heart —
To do, to be,— men's tardy praise to earn,
Their voices called but faintly in his ear;
He only knew " there was so much to learn."
He saw life's plan writ large — the mighty All.
Flesh grew too weak to bind his lofty thought,
And freedom came so gently, without pain,
That we know, some way God gave what he sought.

Somewhere a trumpet calls,— far is the blare.
I hear it on the everlasting hills;
I will stand before God and dry my tears,
(Though now my cup with drearest sorrow fills.)
For our despair and sorrow,— what are they?
If man were shaped all joy, a palsied clod,
He would go down to death and care no more
Than doth the little grass blade on the sod.
Clear and serene my vision on the hills;
Gone is the burning grief I nursed before.
Oh, hold him closely in your hearts, beloved;
He will be lonely, if ye love no more.
Fail not in ministry that once ye knew;

6

Give him the daily thought, the tender needs;
The seraphs cannot wean him from your love.
A poet, and a poet's son: he heeds.

God gave him peace —(we may not know His way)—
The door is shut, and all our mortal breath
But casts a little mist before our eyes;
We may not know the happy ways of death.
But this is sure: if we have lived and loved
As he, and toiled for our small happiness,
We shall move onward toward the open sea;
With all life gave,— for death can bring no less.

W. B. YEATS — READING

Poet, I had not dreamed how you would be,
Thinking you clay as other men, or blind;
Pondering little whence came your magic,
But wishing as I read for Innisfree,
And the bee-music, and the seven green woods,
And the seven stars, and Seven Wise Ones —
Immortals, who were your long lost kindred.

I had not dreamed you — thinking you but clay
As other men are clay — to make me weep
Or laugh, or feel desire for,— this and all
My outgrown selfhood. Suddenly you rose
In the lamps' flare, grave as the dark waters;
Forgetful of each face, sense winged beyond
The preen of curious eyes and whispered praise.
First the recoil: too perfect far, you seemed;
How dared you wear God's image like a gem,
Or lean so white a hand — a poet's hand?

Your hand more like you than your very self;
Your hand more like you than the shadowed eyes
I could not see, but knew imperial suns
Burned in them. Rustled the leaf; then your voice
Came murmuring of " waters and pale lights ";
Murmuring of Dooney and of Innisfree,
And of the ripples singing on the strand.

8

Poet, now thou hast made for me a dream,—
Not of thyself, but of the Mystic Rose
Thou singest, and the Vessel of the Grail.

THE RESURRECTION

(August, 1914)

When the ardor of life is burnt out, and the earth swallowed up in the sea,
When the heavens are shaken with thunders, where then, my Beloved, shall we
Find shelter from storm and confusion, and cover our heads from the blast
That searches the thrones and the kingdoms that were builded up strong from the past?
Where then shall we flee from the fury that shall torture the quiet of skies
That have covered us over in solace with purple pavilions of lies?
Shall I seek you in vain in the whirling of the dark, tumultuous wind,
In the babel of souls that are crying, in the maze of the thoughts of the mind?
Will you stand on the Amaranth stairway with a band of the spirits of light?
Shall I sink like a plummet and find you in the halls of a Stygian night?
The earth that has spun for a moment in the skin of a binding of air,—
The pinch and the snuff of a comet, and it dies in the ultimate flare;
It dies, and a trillion atoms that the Man-god loves as his own

Are dust of the ashes of heaven, on the fields of in-
finity strown.
Where then is the love beyond loving we plighted with
seal of our tears?
Where then are the doubts and the torments of all
of our exquisite years?
And if they are but naught in the heavens when the
fury of death is at hand,
When the sighs and the groans of the dying stir the
heart of the sea and the land,
Where goeth that beauty immortal,— the fire that
burns in the brain?
Can hell swallow that in its scorning? Did Socrates
die, but in vain?
The breath of the rose — has it journeyed as far as
the goal of my bliss?
Do the proud and the humble together fall down in
the angry abyss?
And the Mother of God, and Queen Isis, Astarte,
Astoreth of old,
With Syrinx and Pan and Apollo, and Dian, the hunt-
ress so cold?
Where then is their love and their glory? Did they
die with the glory they made,
When the hurricanes blew in the turrets, when the
temples were rent and decayed?
Is there neither wrath nor forgiving; is there neither
loss nor gain?

At the end of our dervish whirling, does oblivion quiet
our pain?

I will hunt as the Merciless Hunter through the darkness and whirlwinds of space,
Through a thousand hells and heavens, to come to the sight of your face.
And if you are no more than a quiver of light on a heavenly hill
I will mould you again from the æthers; you shall live in the might of my will.
I will clasp you and hold you and bind you by the power of the living God
That is in you, and of you, above you; that lives in the earth that we trod.
And the whirlwinds no more shall subdue me, nor the wrath of the Ancient of Days;
I shall drink from the chalice of Godhood; I shall stand in the heavenly ways,
And freed from the flesh that has perished, a thousand times in the years,
We shall gather our joys and our ardors, our sighs, and the cleansing of tears;
And under our feet the dread whirlwinds, and under our feet broken bars;
And over us glory celestial, and over us radiant stars.

THE FLIGHT

PAST men,
Past their desires,
Past all the murmur of their hurrying feet,
The clangor of the street,
And their hearth fires;
Beyond all hopes and dreams;
Yea, beyond all adventuring at last;
Farther away than Past,
Farther than Future seems —
I fled.

Past vales
Where sweet suspires
Stainless flower-souls in perfume on the air;
Where lily-gardens bear
For the wind-lyres;
Past all quick buds that wake;
Past blasted buds that knew not life or death,
Where mourns the dove, who saith,
" I grieve for thy sweet sake "—
I fled.

Past lust
Where passion tires,
Within the graveyard of the soul's fair faith,
Where First Love's frail wan wraith
Feeds funeral pyres;

Beyond all moon-flung shade;
Yea, far beyond Lust's purple satiate throne,
Where Self seeks Self alone,
Passion by flesh betrayed —
I fled.

Past babes
Whose pureness hires
Us recreant from our heaven back to earth
(They surely have dared birth
For our desires);
Then shall one halt awhile?
Yea, still upon the thundering slopes my feet
Clattered — I heard them beat —
Impatient for each mile
I fled.

Past God,—
That Presence dire,
Shaped by the racial reverence of mankind;
The all deceptive Mind
That set Him higher
Than Man within the skies;
Past monstrous God — yea, past His reeling stars,
His heaven's burning bars,
Past the pale Heaven of Lies
I fled.

14

Past love,
The unquenched fire,
Unto a still cold realm so far remote
That not one singing note
Of love's desire
Its peace could violate,
Where nought is, or is not,— the last outpost
Gained by man's frantic ghost,—
To worlds yet inchoate
I fled.

MOTH FLOWERS

The pale moth
Trembles in the white moonlight;
Thus my heart trembles with love!

The rose petals fall —
The red petals of my heart;
Oh, the breath of love!

Cool, sweet tears
Of honey, the jasmine weeps;
Burning fall the tears of love.

Oh, how bitter
Is the White Poppy, Death;
There are no more dreams of love.

WHO AM I?

Who am I? True, a Seeker, that is sure,—
Drawn hither by the immemorial lure
Of earth-lust ravishing the plastic flesh;
Remembered in the bodiless grey mesh
Of memory's lotos-isle 'twixt life and death —
That dream-world poised aloft 'twixt breath and
breath —
Well I remember that far, lovely land
Where pale Immortals clasped me by the hand;
Where I was god-like. From that clear, bright bliss,
On the will's wings, I sank to the abyss
Of the quick Over-world of lost desire,
Incarnate in spent thought; the astral fire
Circling the planet in mercurial flame; —
Then sinking lower still, to flesh I came.

Who am I? 'Twas for this that martyrs bled,
And men war, dabbling the whole world red,
Answered but by the evil that they make,—
Their Devil, with the world a pawn at stake.
And no man yet has flung the answer even
From out the halcyon slopes of heaven;
And those who challenged down hell's fearful stair
"Who am I?"— only silence answered there.

Who am I? All the searching soul can find
Writ in the illumined missal of the mind;
All that the aspiring mind can climb to see
Within the soul's unplumbed infinity
Answers me not; so, following the Spark,
Naked, I face My Own Law in the dark.

THE WOOD

I HEARD men's voices calling in the street,
Raucous and cold, like ravening birds of prey:
" Lo, passion fades," one cried, " and love
Within earth's mortal climate cannot stay; "
" Alas, all lovely things come to an end; "
" No man can hope to keep his love for aye; "
" Who wins shall lose "—'twas thus the voices cried;
I heard them through the years — and yesterday.

Straight to the Wood — I ran; her covert roof
Whispered with inarticulate, sweet sound;
I plucked a bluebell from the moist warm turf;
I plucked a hazel on a faery mound.
" O fair, strong Wood," I said, " lo, you have held
The secret of content within thy bound;
O quiet Wood, what lure intangible
Draws to thy leafy ways a joy profound? "

Then there was singing in the fluttering leaves;
And there was music of sweet muted lyres;
And through the silence dripped a honeyed voice,
The throaty speech of all the Wood's desires.

" I am the Wood; I seek not anything.
Passion forsakes not power, nor love the soul
That builds its mansion in the Secret Place
Known to itself, nor asks pale beggars' dole."

THE SEAS OF GOD

Lo, there are Seven Seas. The first is dim
With drifting shadows,— dreams that keep
The vision of the Holy Cherubim
Unto the Gate of Birth. In mystic sleep
The tranced mariner holds his way fast
Throughout the shades to freedom and to light,
With his rich argosy won from the past,
And dares to will beyond the enswathing night.

Next is the Sea of Storms; the placid calm
Yields on the instant to the hurricane;
Nor any sacred oil or holy balm
Can still the waves that writhe in hellish pain.
From one pale port all mariners embark;
And no man knows if evil fate, or kind,
Shall cast him living to the ravening shark,
Or fill the sails with many a heavenly wind.
No friendly compass guides the helmsman's hand;
False swings the needle on this wild, strange sea;
Only a mirage of enchanted land
Bids him sail on — until futility
Falls on him like a scourge; the sails rot fast;
The hull, worm-eaten, yields its sacred store;
Fell lightnings shatter every noble mast;
Down sinks the vessel to the ocean's floor,
There for an age within primordial slime
To moulder till the Last Trump sounds the doom.

Then with a spurt, up-rearing from the grime
That binds the living to a rotting tomb,
The mariner shall hail his destiny,
And in new flesh stand forth with awe-struck eyes,
While from God's hand descends a twilight sea,
Blown hither by the winds of Paradise.

Lo, this the Sea of Clouds, low-rolling, vast,
Pale amber, crimson, gleaming amethyst;
Billow the clouds around each straining mast;
And the Sea's emerald is softly kissed
By sun-rays colored by the vapored sense
That on the waves deceptive glories shed,—
Breaking the prism into opulence
That with rare flashings crown the helmsman's head.
No vessel sinks upon this cloud-girt sea,
But all are lost upon its flashing tide
And sail like phantoms cruising ceaselessly
Until the helmsman hath forgot he died
And knows that he drifts toward that far sea-gate
That opens to a soundless clarion
Unto the wider waters of life's fate
Beyond the meadow-vale of Avilion.

Beyond this hard-won gate a Shining Sea,
Placid and golden as a Seraph's smile,
Meets the blue heaven to infinity;
And there fall luscious cadences the while
From out desire's sweet flutes, soft-driven

By the curled images of ecstasy,
Down from the glassy floor of heaven
Upon the Sea, to make sweet minstrelsy.
And the rapt voyager, lulled to sleep,
Dreams on, held in perpetual happy trance,
While his bark slips once more upon the deep,
Full-breasted, careless of the waves' mischance.

Lo, now the Sea of Splendor and of Power,—
The eddying wash of glory and of light
Foams the bark's prow. Here every barren hour
Is wrung into the essence of delight.
The ship flies on; no weaving of the helm
Can bend her course; and the pale mariner,
Giddy with strong soul-breathings that o'erwhelm,
Hears a bell tolling softly in his ear
Whose sound is endless triumph and delight.
Blinded by joy ineffable to every ray
Save his Soul-sun, around him dawns the light
Of the high tide of heavenly ecstasy.

And he has reached the Sea of Blessedness,
That haven of the gods, far, far remote,
Where love dies in a last long peacefulness,
Where life expires in one long singing note.
Where a diviner rapture rends the air,
Leaping in flame; and the ethereal flesh
Dies in unshaping, in the exultant flare,
Tangled at last in God's Immortal Mesh.

22

Last, the Great Sea no man may rightly name
Save as he shadows its white holiness.
Tongue cannot syllable the Word of Flame;
Soul cannot hold the measure of its bliss.
Its tides eternal are God's cleansing blood;
And all who win this Sea before His throne,
Beginning and the *End* have understood;
And thence returning, on swift pinions blown,
Come as Redeemers — Saviors of the Stars —
Sworn to give All — returning to earth's sod —
Banished by the inexorable bars
Of freedom, there to serve the Most High God.

II

SONNETS

THE SOUL'S DESIRE

LOVE does not serve Life's dumb and driven shame;
Nor is Love blind: Love hath all-seeing eyes,
And walks clear-visioned in her Paradise,
And tends nought there save her own altar flame,—
Hears but one sound: Love's immemorial name,—
Knowing Love moveth to itself, and cries
Above the clamor of earth's sense-born lies
Upon each soul within a mortal frame.

Love serveth only Love. Oh, turn away
From dust, my soul, nor seek joy in the clay;
But with Promethean pang usurp thy fate
Of Godhead,— with the Immortal Substance mate:
The unquenchable, ethereal fire —
Creation infinite — the Soul's desire.

COME THOU WITH ME

Come thou with me to that ethereal sphere
Where Love hath wings of fire. Bind not my sense
Unto earth's giddying vapors, that immense
Roll in swart clouds darkly around me here,
Swooning my soul with shapes of deadly fear;
Else flesh to spirit shall make sharp offence
Beyond the dewfall of my penitence,
And Love die bleeding upon Passion's bier.

Come to that stilly heaven far remote,
Where we shall win the ardors of the Sun;
Our ecstasy shall sound a trumpet-note
That to the Holy of Holies forth shall run
Upborne — upon Infinity afloat —
Uniting our two souls unto the One.

THE ASCENT

THROUGH misery infinite, within the wake
Of writhing shadows of forgotten things,
Corpses of murdered dreams, that memory flings
Upon the moving screen, I foothold take
Upon my slippery sins, and for Love's sake
Can stand bolt upright, sloughing all that clings —
Mire of the road — waiting a flame with wings,
A purging fire that my Soul's drought shall slake.

New-born each day, as those who strive with death
On wastrel battle lines, my quaking breath
Draws God's bright seraphs round me pityingly,
Who am so weak, yet still must fight or die;
My destiny foretold . . . angel or clod —
In the end nothing,— or a Son of God.

THE END AND THE BEGINNING

God, I return to Thee! Bruiséd and weak,
Spent with vain tourneying with sin and death,
Fearing that each day's dawn outlast the breath
To bear my body up, I dare to speak
Thy Name, and parting from the world's foul reek,
Lean hard upon Thy mighty word that saith:
" None of thy sins My love remembereth;
I have been flesh,— the lowly and the meek."

God, I return to Thee; make Thou my soul
One golden grain within Thy radiant Whole.
I want no life but as I live in Thee,
Nor heaven save in Thy Infinity;
So wearily my feet each earth-path trod —
To find — the End — and the Beginning . . . God.

IRREVOCABLE

The ghosts of old caresses come to me
Within the pale dawn-light. Thy kisses burn
On other lips than mine; I see thee turn
To alien arms. Oh, never minstrelsy
Sobbed out so lorn a theme by any sea
As wail of longing love that comes to learn
It cannot violate the sealéd urn
Wherein the Past holds fast her constancy.

O God, I want not what another had;
It is the thought that part of you is lost,
That I must ever with forgiveness sad —
Compassion mending life — count still the cost,
And force content with less than what you are;
Gaze at a rush-light, when I dream — a star.

THE END

After my tears, I slept, upon the day
You left me. Some snapt cord brought swift release
From sorrow; and oblivion's dull peace
Fell on my heart; and far and far away
I slipped into a Nowhere dull and grey,
Where all life's troublings on the instant cease,—
Lost in a drifting mist like fierce wild geese
That honk farewell into an ice-bound bay.

I slept to wake, O God, alone — alone;
Flung brutally from out the crypt of sleep,
Instant my soul sped over sea and shore
To the world's end, returning with sad moan,
With unassuaging tears for me to weep,
And the unending wail of "Nevermore."

THE SECOND WIFE SPEAKS

Aye, tell me of those days in Italy
With her; for I would hark the magic strain
That bridehood sings; no premonitioned pain
Warps its great hope that feeds on ecstasy
And thrills with shapes of wonder yet to be.
Measure for me each hour, and once again
Look deep within my eyes, that once were fain
To veil from thee a woman's ardency.

Findest thou not one day that *I* may keep
From out oblivion, where all days run,
Nor yet one leaping hour to make me glad.
Within my breast a poignard stabbing deep,—
That day of days when, proud and all love-mad,
She kissed thy lips and told thee of thy son.

HEARTACHE

Beloved, since love's insight gives to thee
Such power to wound, some secret way to find
The one sad, aching spot within my mind,
That from old custom is not quite set free
(Yet holding promise of some grace to be),
Canst thou not with sweet salve this sore wound bind,
And with a soft excuse be gently kind,
Knowing thou hast my stanchest fealty —

Some healing word, some comfort for my breast,
A talisman that with dull grief can cope,
Soothing, to quiet all my heart's unrest,
Sweeping my mind of every trouble bare,
Writing my name upon a page that's blest,
Emblazoned with the heraldry of hope?

HOPE LIES IN THIS

" Where lieth hope that conquers sullen death?
No argonaut brings tiding of that sea;
Faith's prophecy of splendors yet to be
Gives cold assurance to the tarrying breath."
These are the words that fretfully Love saith
From the Beginning, low, and bitterly,—
Rebellious 'gainst Death's sorrowful decree,
Upon the shores where faint hope wandereth.

" Hope lies in this," an angel bade me speak;
" If with my Love in life I lived and moved
Close — hand to hand — close — touching lip and
cheek,
Thus conquering life with love, our faith is proved;
Life's weaker brother, Death, hath lesser power —
He cannot win from Love a single hour."

THE ANSWER

My babe must wait within the shadows where
Burn souls unborn, dim points of amber flame.
He cannot hear my voice; he has no name
That tongue can syllable upon the air;
His home, alas, it is not here — nor there;
And yet I know that unto me he came,
A blessed spirit free from mortal blame
And all the sorrow that the earth-born bear.

I would not bring him to mortality
To know Promethean pain. Why should he come
(This sun-bright elfin of Eternity),
The depths of all my misery to plumb?
Better that 'twixt me and Desire's hot word
Stood Eden's angel with the flaming sword.

MY NEED

I THOUGHT the world had grown a sombre grey,
The sun burnt out, the stars waxed dim and dead.
I heaped sad curses on my luckless head;
I had been born too late; — the sight of day
Was evil to me, fires burned in my clay,
And ghosts of fears like birds plucked shred by shred
At my still heart, that slowly, slowly bled,
And all desire for life fast ebbed away.

You came to me; you comforted my soul,
And by some healing grace didst make it whole,—
Stanching my life-blood with thy two strong hands
Upon my breast. Then slowly ran the sands
Of life, and I saw what was false, and true —
Death had not been my need, but only you.

MYSTERIES

THERE is one mystery that haunteth me:
Where is the self that I was yesterday?
Where are the thousand selves that fade away
In dim procession in my memory,—
Those strangers who have built my destiny
And bade me go with tears or roundelay,
Where, veiled, the Future waits in distance grey—
Imperious leman of eternity?

And still another mystery is set
Above those yesterdays that I forget:
Visioned within my soul's clear mirror lies
Tomorrow's self. Each night it swiftly flies
Beyond my ken. Unrealized, unseen,
Where goes this shadow-shape—*I might have been?*

THE HIGHEST LOVE

On the high plane of spirit undefiled,
There would I dwell with thee for evermore,
As one who sleeps and dreams far from the roar
Of busy marts; or as a languid child
Muses in summer fields with sighs so mild,
And pensive eyelids, till the day is o'er;
Then half reluctant seeks his natal door,
Sad that from faery shores he is exiled.

Thus would I live in dream and thought of thee,
Free from the weight of any mortal woe;
Shut from the sights and sounds that fetter me;
Held in a current whose resistless flow
Doth bear my spirit close enwrapt with thine,
Commingling our pure love with love divine.

TO "NESITA, SWEET SINGER IN THE TEMPLE OF AMMON"

Thou of old Egypt, from what spicéd tomb
Have alien hands, with ruthless insolence,
Borne here this silent, mocking, brave pretence
Of immortality, this Nilus-bloom,
Withered, and banded in a narrow room?
How still thou art! Time cannot bear thee hence;
Near thee, methinks, the very air is dense
With panoply of shadows in the gloom.

Nesita, singer of an ancient race,
Thebes crumbles, and afar there lingereth
Of Ammon's temple but a storied trace.
Thou art forgot; the old gods yield their breath;
Outworn the Sphinx; but in thy quiet face
One spell survives,— the mystery of death.

FOOLS

If there be aught that dead men think upon
With keen regret, most keen of all is this:
That they went dumbly down the ways of bliss,
Nor knew how glad a thing the world rolls on;
Nor built they for life's joys some Parthenon
Of art's delight, where to enshrine, I wis,
Fame's laurel crown, or love's immortal kiss,—
Immortal with the stars of Orion.

Lo, they are cursed who, having held life's lyre,
Struck not a note, nor let a song suspire
'Twixt lips ensanguined with the blood of God;
These are the little worms beneath the sod,
These are the dumb, blind souls beneath your feet,
The dusty fools who knew not life was sweet.

IDEALA

I LOVE you most when false I seem to be,
For I remember well the olden tale
That of fond lovers one must surely fail
In merit and in tender constancy;
That it is law, one must a traitor be,
And over darkling waves set crimson sail,
Filling to sweep of every wanton gale
That idly blows upon Life's murmurous sea.

I could bear my own falseness, but not thine;
I have seen in your eyes the Flower divine,
The Grail-flower, holy chalice of Christ's blood,
Won by thy purity, thy hardihood.
Profane not holy things; — by love's decree,
If one must sin, oh, let that one be me.

IN GAZA

I

How well those days are writ upon my brain,
Those langorous, purple days brimmed o'er with bliss,
That waking, dreaming held for me but this
Great love that ever mocketh me again.
Through all the darkness of my hours of pain
Still thrills the wonder of her traitor-kiss,
And all the softness of her breast I miss,—
Her dove-like breast, of which I was so fain.
Dark browed are all the women of my race,
And tawny-colored, saffron-like or dun;
She was a miracle, with lily-face
Set in a halo of imprisoned sun,—
A net of sorcery, her flower-like face
That caught my soul, ere our love had begun.

II

But were the way again for me to tread,
Still would I love her, for no mortal man
Since that fair Eden where our time began
Hath had such joy,— the living or the dead,—
Or found such resting place unto his head.
There is no sting of shame, no bitter ban,
Nor gibe nor taunt, nor anything that can
Make me desire aught in this great love's stead.
Imperishable, through my black despair

Weaves in and out the magic of her voice;
I could not kill her, for she was so fair
When round my face fell all her yellow hair,—
A golden cloud that made the eye rejoice,
And sweeter than the fragrance that it bare.

THE LAST VEIL

Men say there are no mysteries any more;
The glades are bare where goat-hoofed Pan held sway;
And all the nymphs and satyrs fled away
Unto a star, where mystery abides,
Swinging englamored in the solar tides;
Vanished the coverts where shy Daphne lay,
Or Dian — and that "Moon-boy" till the day —
Nor any whisper hill to hill confides.

The veils are torn asunder. Nevermore
Shall silence answer from the winding shore
The inarticulate murmur of the sea;
We have made bold to know our destiny.
Yet 'round our altars — to our joy or ruth —
The gods still weave the immortal veil of Truth.

THE GRASSHOPPER

(With apologies to Leigh Hunt and John Keats)

Summer doth bring soft music to our feet,
The droning hum of all her wingéd throng
That sings on sunburnt hills a drowsy song,
With blurring notes and dreamy chirrings fleet,
And amorous mating calls, for summer meet.
And o'er it all soars ever loud and long,
From where he hides the warm, ripe grass among,
The grasshopper's high chant so sharp and sweet.

When to some vagrant summer our thought flies,
And memory, wayfaring, the heart thrills,
Again amid the meadow-sedge he lies,
And at our tread his voice insistent shrills —
Blithe clamorer of summer's ardencies —
The grasshopper chants on remembered hills.

THE RETREAT FROM MONS

1914

YEA, there are many dead, the brave first-born
Of battle, and of England's sons the flower.
Yet dare not weep for them this awful hour;
Keep faith, lest God shall blast ye with His scorn.
The dead ride on; for them Valhalla's horn
Pierces the battle-murk; the grey clouds lower
Beneath their feet, who rise by blood-bought power
To vision on the hills the Eternal morn.

Yea, there are many dead, but dare not weep
For English men. Only the bodies sleep;
Their souls ride on. Above the entrenched host
Battalions wheel, and each avenging ghost
Fights on for England. Hark, high overhead
The drums of glory marshall forth the dead.

TO ROOSEVELT

WHO does thee justice in a grimy world?
Not he who blackens thee as spawn of hell,
Clutching at lies, and drifting on the swell
Of mad ambition, that with shame unfurled
Drives on to ruin, by foul currents hurled
Of thine own nature; nor doth he do well
Who paints thee saint-like in a priestly cell,
Counting thy beads with valorous deeds empearled.

The hoarse mob-voice can never make nor mar
Thy destiny. Heed not its venomed rage;
Beyond the crowds grave Justice scans afar,
Writes all thy sins and virtues on her page;
Then turns her eyes upon Truth's guiding star,
And knows thee, Great-Heart, in a stormy age.

SLEEP

When I have fought with pain a weary space
And, feverish, disdained the breast of Night,
Waiting for dawn to bring the peering light,.
Thou comest, Sleep, with grave and hallowed pace,
Sifting dull opiate; thy embowered face
Smiles on me with forgetfulness of sight;
Thy breath a fragrant gale, that in its flight
Brings spiced balm pain's writing to efface.

Fold me within thy shadows to repose;
Strew as the summer sward with leaf of rose
Thy golden dreams. Then will I humbly pray
One boon, the last, ere thou dost haste away;
In thy oblivion steeped, lulled by thy breath,
Deliver me to thine own sister, Death.

SONGS, BALLADS, PASTORALS

THE FAERY WOMAN

Come back, my Faery Mistress,
From out the Tullach hills.
I miss thy wild, sweet singing
That all my being thrills.

I want thy faery fingers
To rest upon my brow,
When through the blackened branches
The night winds call and sough.

Come dance upon the headlands
And crags along the sea,
And those black rocks shall softer
Than meadows seem to me.

Thou'rt wilful and thou'rt wanton;
Thy smile is wan as mist;
But blessed he of mortals
Who once thy lips has kissed.

On nights when mortals slumber,
Upon the window ledge
The faeries weave the moonbeams
Into a magic bridge.

And who would out and follow
Must pass as he was born
Upon the path of moonlight,
Else he must wake forlorn.

For all the greed of living
His soul must lay aside,
To woo a faery woman,
To win her for his bride.

But once his eyes have quickened
To meet her dancing 'een,
No more doth memory haunt him
With all that might have been.

So come, my Faery Mistress,
My heart dies in my breast.
Thy feet must dance before me
Ere my soul finds its rest.

I blind my eyes to seek thee,
And all my senses find
Is but a ghostly murmur,
A whisper on the wind.

SCOTCH ARRAN

Oh, I would like to tread once more
The weedy strand of Arran's shore,
And I would like to set my feet
Down where the sand and heather meet.
And once again in rocky glen
I'd like to meet with faery men,
Chasing the white does through the mist.
But more than all, oh, I would list
A voice that called me by my name,
Shot through the air like holy flame.
Then I forgot the things that seem,
And wandered in a happy dream;
And saw a door that opened wide,
Set in the craggy mountain side;
And knew that joy for ever more
Was just the other side the door,
And I should walk with Aengus there,
And Etain of the yellow hair.

Oh, would that I could tread once more
That weedy strand, that heather shore.

THE RAINS OF ARRAN

'Tis not the Arran sunshine
I'm loving best of all,
But the little rains of Arran
That suddenly do fall
From out the breast of heaven,
At morning and at eve,
To fill the thirsty veins of earth
And hush the winds that grieve:
With gentle pitter-patter,
The winds for ever more
To hush within the heather
That loves the Arran Shore.

I'd wandered far from mercy
And farther still from grace,
But I found a tongue for praying,
Arran's rains upon my face.
And in the dusk and coolness
Of Sannox' lonely Glen,
In the silver rain of Arran,
I found my soul again.

"RIDERS TO THE SEA"

Six we were who rode away
    Down to Kildonan.
We heard the neighing of the spray
That raced the wind by night and day
    Beyond Kildonan.

Six we drove 'fore a swaying mast,
    Out from Kildonan.
Six our bones to the sea-wolves cast;
None returned at the very last
    Unto Kildonan.

Fast in the wrack of storms we flew
    Far from Kildonan.
The cables snapt; the mermen knew
Where we slept in the caverns blue
    Far from Kildonan.

Never a dripping plank for rest
    Out from Kildonan.
The priest said mass to east, to west,
And, "The good God, He knoweth best,
    Here in Kildonan."

SONGS OF BALLYSHANNON

I

TAKE me home to Ballyshannon, for there's music in the word;
The name o' Ballyshannon is the sweetest ever heard!
The little hills are lying fair and green behind the town,
And the skies of Ballyshannon, why, they're never known to frown.
Take me back and let me hearken to the plaintive Irish wind;
Take me back to Ballyshannon, where the neighbors' hearts are kind.

I will wander in the moonlight out upon the ragged moor,
With the flaming gorse and heather,— I'll not find it mean or poor.
In the glen with lads a-dancing, I will pass the night away;
For the nights in Ballyshannon, they are sweeter than the day.
Take me back to Ballyshannon, there's a voice that calls to me;
For my heart's in Ballyshannon on the other side the sea.

II

I came to Ballyshannon on a wet and mournful night,
And all the way was darkness, with never a ray of light;
The mist was waving 'round me and the winds were blowing free
When I came to Ballyshannon, sure my heart was whole in me.

I went from Ballyshannon when the sun was rolling high,
And every rowan bud was glad and looked me in the eye;
The clouds were white above me and the winds played in the tree,
Yet I went from Ballyshannon bearing little heart in me.

Sure, my heart was crushed and broken; there were kisses on my mouth;
There were cruel words upon me like a summer's parching drouth.
Woman's wiles are full of mystery, they're inconstant as the sea;
Just for sport in Ballyshannon, someone stole the heart of me.

III

The bells o' Ballyshannon, I hear them on the wind,
And every care and sorrow my heart leaves far behind;
I can live and thrive a season upon an alien shore,
But I'm wanting Ballyshannon forever all the more;
And when light o' life has left me and I'm like an empty byre,
Lay my bones in Ballyshannon, take me back to heart's desire,
Where I'll hear the bells a-ringing, folded arms beneath the sod,
For the bells of Ballyshannon, they will ring me home to God.

Oh, the little waves are beating upon Ireland,
They are crying out their pain along the shore,
And a long farewell I'm giving
To the hope of all my living,
(Mavourneen, I shall never see thee more.)

Oh, the little waves are sighing upon Ireland
They are wailing all along the dreary shore
And I watch the hills receding
All my heart within me bleeding,
(Mavourneen, I shall never see thee more.)

All the tears of mourning eyes in Erin's country
They have wept their bitterness upon the sea;
All the land is filled with sorrow;
There is never joy tomorrow,
And the burden of their woe lies black on me.

Oh, the little waves are beating upon Ireland,
They are moaning all around the dreary shore.
(Spindrift like thy hair is blowing,
Happiness I'm no more knowing,
Mavourneen, I shall never see thee more.)

THE STRANGER IN THE GLEN

Now who was walking in the glen?
" It may ha' been the sojer men."
Nay now, Nora Creena,
One came on lepping fast and free
With eyes like flowerets drowned at sea,
And all his glances were for thee,
Nora Creena.

Now who came up the byre road?
" It may be it was Father Brode."
Nay now, Nora Creena.
I heard one dance, I heard one sing
Like faerie in a magic ring;
Say who should dare so bold a thing,
Nora Creena?

Now who knocks at thy lowly door?
" Maybe a stranger from the moor."
Nay now, Nora Creena.
I heard a bow shaft sting the air;
The Archer Love is standing there;
Ah, brush the floor, for him prepare,
Nora Creena.

You hear him knocking now so loud.
" Does Love come humble-like or proud?"
Say now, Nora Creena?

Alack, the door swings open wide;
What spectre this that stalks inside?
'Tis Death, not Love, will win my bride,—
Nora Creena.

THE BITTER HERB

O BITTER herb, Forgetfulness,
I search for thee in vain;
Thou art the only growing thing
Can take away my pain.

When I was young, this bitter herb
Grew wild on every hill;
I should have plucked a store of it,
And kept it by me still.

But, oh, I plucked the roses;
My heart they cannot heal —
The velvet, crimson roses,
'Tis only joy they feel.

And oh, I plucked the gay flowers,
And scorned the herb of grief;
I scorned the rosemary and rue;
I scorned the bitter leaf.

And now I cast them from me,
The lovely springtime flowers;
They have no solace for my heart,
Nor comfort for my hours.

I hunt through all the meadows
Where once I wandered free,
But the rare herb, Forgetfulness
It hides away from me.

O bitter herb, Forgetfulness,
Where is thy drowsy breath?
Oh, can it be thy seed hath blown
Far as the Vales of Death?

HARBLEDOWN

In Harbledown the churchtower stands
Upon the ancient Roman lands,
And every stone with age is greyed
In the old crypt the Romans made.
Winding the highroad rambles down,
Beyond, to Canterbury town,
Circling the vine-clad belfry tower
That knells the passing of the hour.

Within the close the dead folk sleep,
So happily, one may not weep.
Life's mortal combat passed and gone,
They sleep with heavenly armor on,
Dreaming within the mellow clay
Till Gabriel blows the Judgment Day.

I walked among the grassy mounds;
From out the posies came sweet sounds
Of fluttering wings. A grave-bed stirred;
I saw a soul change to a bird
And seek the utmost parapet
Of that old tower with ivy set;
Then o'er the Sanctuary high
It lost itself within the sky.

I looked beside the mildewed walks,
And found a grave with lily-stalks

Fast withering,— one so lately made
The turf with clay was overlaid.
And where the lilies' whiteness spilt,
A word was traced in silver-gilt:
"*Mavis*"; so then I knew that I
Had seen a bird fly to the sky.

THE FAIRY PRINCE

He came at last — the Fairy Prince,
The God of Dreams — the dim ideal;
But not for me his armor's clang,
And not for me the trumpet's peal.

Within the lists he rode at ease,
A careless victor, lance at rest;
But not for me the tourney won,
And not for me the final test.

His mistress was a spotless maid.
The rose she cast was " Rose o' Youth,"
Even as mine; but my own rose
With drooping leaves revealed the truth.

My feet had known no cloistered path;
From crown to toe I bore the stain
Of contact with the grimy world;
The blot will not come out again.

He came at last — the Fairy Prince;
Across the tourney's lists he passed;
And not for me the laurels won,
And not for me his lance was cast.

But still he came, O God of Dreams
And God of Pain,— he came — *he came.*
His mistress knows him as a man;
I know the Saint who heals my shame.

SONG

FAR, and farther, and far away —
  " Follow — follow "—
For ever, and a year and a day,
While the youth o'thee will stay,
And the blood be calling —
  " Follow — follow "—
Hollow — hollow reeds
You're blowing, Pan.
" Hasten while ye can."

Up and on to the rim of the hill —
  " Follow — follow "—
There is a star, and the wind's sweet will
To guide you on; you may drink your fill
Where the springs are falling.
  " Follow — follow "—
Hollow — hollow reeds
You're blowing, Pan.
" Hasten while ye can."

Just where the hilltop's swaying sedge
  " Follow — follow "—
Touches the sky is the moon's great edge,
Tethered there like a golden sledge,

Where Pan's pipes are calling
" Follow — follow "—
Hollow — hollow reeds
You're blowing, Pan.
" Hasten while ye can."

INDIAN SUMMER

We held our breath lest the bright day should end,
So amber clear its dawn, so blue its noon;
Over the grass still green the dead leaves blew
Rustling reproach that frost should come so soon;
A scent of smoke had drifted through the air;
The sun of afternoon burned through a haze
That sifted o'er each far horizon's edge
In reminiscence of spring's flower-shod ways.

Almost it seemed the morning's dawn would bring
The crocus through its bed of leafy mold;
Almost that tulip beds would flaunt once more
Their piebald silks of crimson and of gold,
And that the larch trees would be rimmed with green,
And maple buds turn red with fragrance sweet,
And all the evanescent, fragile charm
So shortly past lie spread about our feet.

We walked out through the sedge grass, past the marsh,
And finding driftwood cast upon the beach,
Sat watching white-sailed ships that veered along
Full set, some haven of the west to reach.
Among the sedge grass there are roses blown
When summer trails her lovely robe of green
Among the marsh pools, vagrant wildling blooms
That hide behind the grasses' waving screen.

One rose was left that, braving cruel winds,
Gave tardy blossoms by some trick of fate.
Pale blooms we plucked and held against our hearts,
Cherished them dearer that they came so late.
The sun sank downward through the mellow haze
And crimson flared in setting o'er the sky,
As if the day a pensive swan-song wove
In notes of color ere it paled to die.

Soon faded red to amber, rose to gold,
And gold to purple; in the distant west
There shone a clear light not of sun nor moon;
The trees lay silhouetted dark at rest;
Hushed were the birds, a chill was in the air;
One solitary snowflake drifted by,
And in the east the star of evening glowed,
A point of light upon the sombre sky.

O Indian Summer of our northern climes!
O late, wan summer — to our frost-touched hearts!
Something within thee that the spring has missed
The hidden flood-tide of our spirit starts;
Something within thee speaks of purer skies
Where parting comes not, where day doth not cease,
And dust of dead earth roses blooms again
In an immortal summer's perfect peace.

THE WILD ROSE

I AM the Rose outside the garden wall;
You, who are human, hear my little plaint.
The wind is fickle, he remembers nought;
And Philomel — the world calls him a saint —
He loved me once; but other roses bloomed
And he loved them. Perhaps he loves us all;
But Time waits not. In dust we're soon entombed
And vanished; only the strong root remains
That reaches down into the living sod —
Down farther than the creeping winter frost
Can come. There's rose-dust in each clod,
And God and I make roses every year.
We give them to the beggars in the lanes;
We give the children all the buds they ask;
Sometimes when careless summer quickly wanes
We give them to the wind and to the weed.

One grief is mine: I am outside the wall.
At first I did not know, and thought the world
Just weeds and brambles. Then I grew so tall
I could look over in the garden there
At tended flowers, at many a bordered aisle
Set with pale lilies and with every bloom
That's rare and precious. Then a little while
I saw the gardener digging at the briars,
Tying one here, bending another there,
Pruning the recreant shoots that spread too far,

Rearing them smooth and straight and tall and fair.
There were no earth-grubs gnawing at their roots;
They were too precious; service was their meed.
I wondered if the gardener ever knew
The Wild Rose springs from just the selfsame seed.

But there came others to this garden plot;
A Lord and Lady breathed the mellow air.
The Lady held the roses to her breast
And nestled them within her fragrant hair;
And once she turned and saw me bending o'er
The wall, strait-gazing, love in all my crown
Of petals, and the blithesome Lady said,
" My Gardener, you must cut that Wild Rose down."
Perhaps the gardener loved wild roses or perhaps
Forgot the task. I know he never came,
And I clung closer to the rough-hewn wall,
Bowing my head for fear of further blame.

I have the sunlight and the soughing wind
And blowing mists and savor of sea-rain,
And I wax lustily with all my shoots;
And yet there's nought can take away the pain,—
I am outside the wall. There is no converse sweet
With sister-roses,— they who call me " wild "
Who am more tame than they, more meek at heart,
Having no pride to make me less than mild.

The bramble grows my brother, pricks my blooms
With roughness, and the envious thistle hides
Beneath my branches; there the sedge grass grows.
I have fought with them and my strength abides.
A painter sat beside me one whole day,
Praised many a bud and on the canvas drew
My roses, then he turned and went away
Into the garden where my rivals grew.
And once a lover pining for his love
Sang rondels to " a rose " in my green shade;
A wild rose might not serve his love to please,
And yet might give the rondel that he made.

If there are gardens in that happy land
That wise men dream lies at the end of life,
Beyond the bramble and the thistle's stings,
Beyond the pain and all our weedy strife,
I pray the Gardener takes the weary seed
Of all my roses, and that He may find
One seed among them all that He will plant
Within His garden with the gentle kind
Of roses. Then no more my leaves shall make
A trembling sound of sorrow in the night.
Not vagrant, wild, I shall grow tall and straight
As other roses in the Gardener's sight.

TO MY MOTHER

Mother — Mother —
Little Mother mine,
Every year upon your birthday morning
I have sung in rime
Some gay rondelay for love's adorning;
But this gray spring time
I have neither chant nor rondel; their light measures
Vanished from my casket of bright treasures
Long ago. This year the world is weary,
Peace departed —
And my rimed words are sad and dreary.
Heavyhearted
Pass the days in some pale dream of living;
Hope is weary of her endless giving,
And I have no grace of flaunting praises
For thy years.
One gift only, poor but precious,— only —
Only tears
Sobbed out lonely midnights to your soothing,
Tears that we
Wander lost within a maze of horror,
Where Infinity
Pours her cup of blood and wrath and passion,
Vents her antique wrath in newer fashion,
Pouring — pouring blood and souls of men
To some darkling purpose; and again

Our eyes look on dully while our brothers perish.
Irony beyond the grief we cherish,—
We must turn and live, and follow after
All the mocking sweet lure of life's laughter.
I repine
To you in my ashen words, yet must go seeking
Anodyne
In the lees of pleasure: I must bid you close
Your deep vision, seek but color of the rose;
Laugh with me soon in Spring's fragrant netting,
Join me in delectable forgetting.
Mother — Mother —
Little Mother mine,
I will bring you gladness for the asking
All the years;
But today accept this bitter wine,
For today mirth may not be my tasking,—
Only tears.

WILD TANSY

Around the dump heap's ragged edge,
  Within the vacant lot,
The sweet wild tansy grows as free
  As in some sylvan spot.

It creeps around the motley pile,
  A rim of fragrant green;
The fairest thing upon the morn
  That tired eyes have seen.

It does not pine for solitude,
  Nor heed the city's roar,
But lifts its head as buoyantly
  As by some poet's door.

It takes the sunshine from God's hand,—
  This odorous, simple weed;
With sun and rain its faith is sure:
  He knows its every need.

O humble tansy, growing there
  Amid the filthy scum,
A gentle sermon thou dost preach,—
  Although thy leaves are dumb.

THE NOVEMBER DANDELION

November flower, in fields of brown,
I spied thy nodding, golden crown,
A glittering straggler mid the fern
That withered by a frosty burn.
Imprudent flower, couldst thou not learn
The lesson I so often spurn,
Nor spread thy petals to the blast,
Whose every breath might be thy last?

Thou must not pine in meadow drear
In the late Autumn of the year.
I'll pluck thee from untimely fate
To my sad heart; thou art the mate
Of some late hope, whose amber star
Shines with a glamour borne afar,
And claims the shelter of my breast
With thee, sweet posy, sore distressed.

THE DAUGHTERS OF THE RAIN

BETWEEN the darkness and the dawn
Three sisters came to me;
They were the Daughters of the Rain
That dance upon the lea.

They glided o'er my window sill
And 'round my lowly bed,
And placed their cooling hands upon
My hot and aching head.

And one was called Forgetfulness,
And one was Dreamless Sleep.
Beneath her fragrant fingertips
My eyes forgot to weep.

The last was snooded with wet flowers
From green and bloomy sod;
She was the fairest of the three:
Her name was Peace o' God.

Between the darkness and the dawn
They came to comfort me,
The Faery Daughters of the Rain
That dance upon the lea.

RENASCENCE

Tell me, folk of the spring,
Of the flaunting gold and the tender green,—
You who return with insolent tread,
Gladsome of mien,

When will Margery come,
Who folds her hands in the cool dark ground?
Will she dance forth with a gay young smile
From her low mound?

Yield me your secret lore,
How the dust can hold through the brumal night,—
Fragrance and splashings of color that seem
Born of the light?

Emerald, amber and gold,—
Silent you are 'neath the sun and the rain;
The round of a year will your petals fling
Wine-stained again.

And I know she will come
After the winter of death, and its sleep,
With the blue-veined flesh, and the calm, sweet brow,
My love to keep.

Listen, beneath the sod:
In a newer age and a fairer clime
Spring shall be yours and the selfsame eyes,
Margery Mine.

THE BRIDAL

She bade us robe her as a bride
  In satins white and cold,
And crown her brow with rarest gems,
  Though she was very old.

"Today," she said, "the Bridegroom comes,
  And I would fain prepare
To greet him in my bridal pomp,
  That he may find me fair."

She bade them make her room a bower
  Of lily and of rose,
And dress for her a bridal feast
  With every flower that blows.

When all was done, a miracle
  Had washed Time's toil away;
Her cheek was smooth and fresh and fair
  As on her bridal day.

She bade soft music fill the air;
  The door swung open wide;
The Bride rose up to meet the Groom,
  In beauty glorified.

We could not see him as he passed,
  And bore her soul away
To a celestial marriage bed —
  She died upon that day.

TO A PAINTING OF A YOUNG GIRL CALLED "A FLOWER"

Did your beauty only last
One brief hour,
Sweet, that men should name you this —
Just "A Flower"?

You were hardly woman, Sweet,
Just a child;
You were a white rose-bud, Sweet,
Undefiled.

There is not a hint of love
In your face,
Only innocent, wide-eyed
Childish grace.

Yet you seem all formed for love,
Dreamy-eyed;
I could fancy ere I breathed
That you sighed.

Sweet, you were too fair for us,—
Just a flower,
Born to bend and bud and bloom
In a bower.

Like a rose to bud and bloom
And to die,
On a zephyr's vagrant breath,
Shattered lie.

THE AWAKENING

I WAS so young and free and wild,
Nature's own blest and happy child,
Until within Life's ripening wheat
I spied my Mind hid, fast asleep.
For years my Mind has sleeping lain,
While others reaped the ruddy grain.
I struck brute blows in heedless rage;
I cursed the wheat; I cursed the Age,
Since I had gained nought for mine own
Than poppies that the wind had sown.

My Mind awoke and looked at me,—
Below us lay the waving sea
Of ripening sheaves,— then strode away,
And with the reapers every day
Toiled as a Titan. Years fled fast
And all the harvest mine at last.
Alas, my folly and my pain,
Who cannot be care-free again
And glean the poppies from the wheat
And let my Mind forget to reap.

LOVE'S REALITY

I SAID, "If I put all the passion and the pain
Of life into my song, say, who will care to read?
There is so much of joy that waits a word
To sow it broadcast where the world hath need,
Why should I sing the bitter fountain's spurt
Within my heart?" The "*Sedges*" answered me.
(I walked among them that day pondering
On the great bliss of Love's Reality.)

The singing Sedges answered me: "Bend low,
And hark *our* song. We harp-strings of the wind
Sing ever sadly; sedges mourn and mourn
With murmurous music sorrowful, yet kind,—
The soughing sound of peace unspeakable
That calls thee to that last, still resting place
For tired hearts, where droopingly we bend
And with root-tendrils clasp thy quiet face.

"When thy sad songs arise, Old Memory
Stirs from her sleep, and once again thine eyes
Regretful-turning pierce the Veils of Time
And fine that *We* and *Thou* are only *Lies*."
Thus spoke the Sedges by the ragged marsh,
Singing together like a weary sea;
But I climbed to the hills that lay beyond,
And sang my song of Love's Reality.

ASSURANCE

If we can but be true —
Apart, torn by our twain conflicting lives,
Fettered by custom, bound with duty's gyves,
Treading a path of pain, that justice still
Be done on earth as is God's gracious will;
If we can but be true and stem the tide,
Why, He will keep us ever side by side.

If we can bravely love —
No deepest deep unknown, no highest height
We have not won, oh, we shall find the light.
Beyond the lingering hell we dare to scorn
Our hope forecasts a far diviner morn:
If we can bravely love, beside some sea
God will prepare a place for you and me.

And we shall surely know —
All that our hearts have longed for in the years
We toiled and laughed and sang above our tears
And kept clean-hearted in the teeth of wrong,
Whispering each other, " O my love, be strong ":
And we shall surely know whence came the ray
Of purest love that led us all the way.

THE PIXIE'S POOL

I KNEW at once it was a Pixie's Pool,
And that the wood was an enchanted wood,
It was so quiet. There was not a sound
To break the stillness, and I feared to breathe
Lest all might vanish and my eyes awake
On the familiars of our mortal world.
I said there was no sound, yet to the sense
That's hidden, there was chiming of faint bells
As if a moon-moth's wing had swept the tongues
Of the red columbines that fringed the pool,
Or as of elfin laughter echoing far
Within the trumpet stalks, melting to air
Upon the fragrance of their balmy breath.

I laid me down upon the sere brown leaves,
Pierced by the spurring, pale-green shoots of spring,
And watched the shadows pass within the pool,
The flying clouds, the happy, swift-winged birds.
Then from the silence spoke a Spirit-voice:
" This is the mirror of Love's Faeryland,
Where dreams awake from out their life-long sleep."

TO A ROSE TREE

(That bloomed beneath Anne Boleyn's Tudor Rose carved in stone on King's Chapel, Cambridge)

O ROSES of the Tudor time,
These roses of the summer's prime
Emboss their crimson leaves beside
The roses for which men have died.
I grant the Tudor rose its place,
Set by the mullioned window space;
But oh, how heavenly 'tis to me
To pluck a red rose from the tree
That mocks the Tudor Rose so rare
And lives and thrives in common air!

INTERLUDE

Beloved, we'll play together!
Fame's a feather;
Only God and the wind know whether
'Twill settle on river or vale or hill,
But the heart leaps on when the mind is still;
So Love, in the sunny weather,
Come, let us play together.

Beloved, we'll rest a season!
(Needs no reason).
Our souls are free from spot and treason;
The earth will yield us a place for sleeping
When the dark comes on. Dear, to my keeping,—
Your hand; joy will serve as a reason;
Come, let us rest for a season.

Beloved, while yet we have breath
We'll fear not death;
'Tis some false word that the preacher saith.
Down in the long grass Death could not find us,
Where the flame-red lips of the poppies blind us;
Hiding there, we will laugh at Death,—
'Tis a word the preacher saith.

OUR LADY OF THE RAIN

I WILL go to my sweet Lady of the Rain —
I will turn my face and follow where she goes,
And my heart shall lose its longing and its surging, weary pain,
As a mountain in the springtime sheds its snows.

I will go to my sweet Lady of the Rain
As a child, so I will whisper on her breast;
I will fold my tired eyelids where no shadow of disdain
Hides to mock me as I pause a while to rest.

I will go to my sweet Lady of the Rain
With the sorrow born of loving in her eyes,
And the coolness of her fingers where the early flowers have lain
Shall recover me from sickness of life's lies.

I will go to my sweet Lady of the Rain —
O'er the meadows lying verdant we shall tread;
We shall find a hidden well-spring, one for which my heart is fain;
We shall listen, hearing all that could be said.

I will go to my sweet Lady of the Rain —
And together in the silence of the night
She will lead me 'neath wet branches that will drip and drip again
On my feverish eyelids, weary of all sight.

AT THE END

Now there are left at the end only these three:
Wind of the hills, and the blowing rain,
And my great Mother, the Sea.

Lo, Love came, and I heard him beat at the gate,
But kinder the desolate wind
That blows in the salt sea strait.

Lo, Fame cried me; she shone like a moon-struck gem,
But dearer the drops of the summer rain
To make me a diadem.

Lo, God leaned down and caught at the soul of me;
I foreswore God and the Seraphim
For my great Mother, the Sea.

MOONRISE

The dark was velvet, smooth and palpable
And pungent, warm with lily-musk and wine
Of o'er-blown roses mellowed by the sun.
It flowed in waves, soft-beating tides of gloom;
It broke against me in a soundless wash
Of blackness, pouring down a rayless night
Upon my eyelids, swathing me around
With dull oblivion; steeping every sense
To drooping numbness with narcotic calm.

The eyebrow of the moon shot o'er the hill,
And one long lashing of celestial light
Ravished the earth with splendor, silvering
The garden slope unto a shining sea.
With that first ray of light the hush was gone,
(Hid under darkness's wing it fled the spot)
And from the aisles of lily and of rose
There shrillėd clear an ambuscade of pipes
And tinkling bells; the dew began to rise;
And shot from moon-rayed dells and twinkling flowers
There came Titania's host to cry the moon
With argent cymbals and with echoing horns
And all the pomp and pride of Faeryland.

SONG

Beloved, I would sing. Such melodies
Lurk in each bloom that springs along my path;
I would cross hands upon my breast and sing
For gladness, though the song be none of mine,
But borrowed from the haunts of silver rills
And wildwood coverts, sweet with hidden flowers,—
The soft, low sound that summer meadows croon,
Or that the moonflower all the livelong night
Breathes to the moon in dreamings of delight.
I would sing rose-songs. Did you never know
Those perfect blossoms carry in their hearts
Such haunting strains as only Syrinx blew?
If you but listen (with the inner ear)
Over a rose leaf softly, you shall hear
The echoing over-tone that stains the leaf
From palest tint to glowing passion-red.
If I could form in living melody
The deathless beauty that these roses hold,
Could I sing all, then happy it might be
That " I " would vanish and the song would live.

THE MIRACLE

" DEAR Lord," I prayed, " a miracle, and I believe."
Then lo, a-sudden, 'mid the rime of wintry ways
A thorn tree bloomed with tender green of leaf,
And scent that spread upon the sharp, keen air
Like incense blown from some Elysian mead.
Then as I gazed with reverent, wondering eye,
The white bloom vanished, and against the sun
Hung but the bare, black boughs, frost rimmed,
Clashing together in the chilling blast.

" Lord, Thou hast mocked me," loud I cried;
" Thy miracle a mirage of the air,—
A fantasy of brain, now quickly gone.
No sense-deceit can guide my faltering faith.
Grant thou a miracle, and I believe."

Somewhere a Voice spoke, soft and sorrowful:
" There are no miracles, O Son of Man.
That which thou sawest was as real as these
Wild winds that harshly sweep about thy path,
Or yonder bough reft of its fragrant bloom.
Only a moment may the mortal sense
Attune itself to the transcendent sphere;
One fleeting moment may the mortal mind
Mirror the things of spirit without fault.
The green young leaf, the petals flowering white
Realities; but to thy blinded eyes
The wintry snow heaps on the bare, black thorn."

DAISIES

Sometimes I think if I could lie
Among the daisies, underneath June's sky,
I would not ask more of my life than this:
The simple portion of a daisy's bliss.
I would not ask more than the white
And gold that soothes my jaded, weary sight;
Mayhap some playful child would pass my way
And pluck me "just a daisy" for his play;
Or to a love-lorn maid would fall my lot
To answer, "He loves me" or "He loves me not."
Ofttimes I think if there are garlands hung
Around His throne, and snowy blossoms flung
For the swift passing of the angels' feet,
Those flowers of Heaven, wonderful and sweet,
Are but the souls of daisies pure and white,
Transplanted to those realms of radiant light.

AVALON

If you, dear heart, in lands that lie
Beneath the ever changeful sky
Have found a city, wondrous fair,
Called Avalon, oh, tell me where?

It was so very long ago —
How many years I do not know —
I passed without its portals fair,
And turned to find — but empty air.

Long have I searched, but searched in vain,
To find those magic gates again;
But ever they lie far away
Beyond the rippling edge of day.

But sometimes in the morning dim,
When wild birds chant their matin hymn,
I see her towers in vision rise,
A misty mirage in the skies.

Sometimes when dreaming half awake,
I rest beside some woodland lake,
From out its depths in splendor gleams
The long-lost city of my dreams.

And sometimes in thy voice I hear
Her bells that ring so sweet and clear;
And in thine eyes of blue I see
A wraith of my lost Arcadie.

Her bells ring out so glad and free;
Her banners stream full merrily;
But never more shall these two feet
Tread lightly her enchanted street.

Fair is the rose you gave to me,
But fairer those I ne'er shall see;
Though bright the sun shines down today,
My Avalon lies leagues away.

When still I lie at last, and dead,
And from this flesh the soul has fled,
Mourn not nor weep for what is gone:
It dwells in peace in Avalon.

THE BLAZONED ROSE

THE ECHO

THERE are sounds so beautiful that they seem to be the sounds of heaven. There is the sound of a lily bursting its sheath; there is the sound of the wind in the grass; there is the sound of the far-away brook in the woodland, the sound of the sea, the whisper of the breath softly inhaled and exhaled by lovers. But more wonderful, more beautiful than all is that mysterious murmur that fills my mind with awe, and my soul with reverence, the sound of the beating of your heart. To lie upon your breast, to listen to the muffled pulsations — knowing how near and yet how far one life is from another — fills me with strange speculations. I lose at times the sense of being alive. I am dead, and your heart is beating over me,— will always be beating over me. I was born only to hear that sound; I shall go on forever hearing it, a calyx, a wall against which the throbs pulse. And I give back the beat: I am the echo of your heart. When you have dreamed, I have watched the fluttering of the white flesh, the tiny ripple that marked systole and diastole, and thought that if your heart ceased to beat my own heart would stop — would die as an echo dies. And if my body still lived, it would live without a heart, for the beat of your heart moves mine.

REFUGE

I TAKE refuge in a great love.
Out of the wrack and ruin of life
There appears to me a shape of splendor —
Love-glorious, all compelling —
Love-deathless and everlasting —
The exalted worship of the soul,
The mystic worship of the body,
Filling the universe,
Surrounding its object
With perfection;
Asking only perpetuation as reward,
Only delight in the burning
That destroys the tares of life
And lifts the reedy fluting of earth-voices
To celestial music.

I take refuge in this great love;
It is my sanctuary;
It is the bosom of God
From whence I came,
To which I have been eternally returning.

THE SOUL'S ELECT

Beyond possession, I possess you, having come
Unto the Holy Temple — to your Soul, which Time
Hath now restoréd me, like as the sense-cloyed air,
Unto a poet yearning, the forgotten rime
His song but lacked.
Nay, come not near, nor touch me now;
Thou art my Well-Beloved; there can never be
Between us love's profaning; for the Eternal Flame
Hath caught us living to God's holy mystery.
I burn as Danaë in the Shower of Gold;
Yet virgin to thee, I shall bear immaculate
The Son of God. Lo, now, He stirs beneath my heart,
And in my dream afar the Mages watch and wait.

WE ARE NOT TWAIN

We are not twain: hell is duality,
And blessed Oneness all the heaven to find.
I grow in thee. Dost thou not feel each vein
Throb fullness with my life? Oh, rich and pure,
Its fountains feed thee, welling from my heart —
Supreme surrender and supreme desire.
All that thou art springs fecundate in me;
All thou couldst win clings close upon my pride;
All I aspire thy Wholeness doth outpour
Upon my spirit in high ecstasy,
And our Souls' Self in darkness whispereth:
" I am thy God; there is no other God! "

RESIGNATION

Love, I have lost so many of your years
That I give up, lose heart, and let you go.
You have lived out your life, and I may sue
The years in vain, and hear the clanging, "No,"
Answer desire. Yes, I shall give you up,
Resign myself to duty's patient lies,
And spill forgetfulness from the bright cup
Of youth. Alas, that there are none so wise
They can bring back to me your youthful days
That are no more. "Alas, this day and this,"
I cry; "they ran so joyous down life's ways;
I know, I know how much of you I miss."

Had I been with you in each fond, lost dream,
I should have grown as fair as Deirdre,
Who loved in the green wood beside the stream,
Till Death grew jealous of her liberty;
I should have drunk thy loving breath by breath,
While each slow moon her hollow crescent filled;
I should have prayed thy love might bring me death
Ere the quick rapture of our days was stilled.
I am resigned — O God, forgive the lie.
There is a world set over sun and moon,
Beyond the azure empire of the sky,
And there, I pray Thee for a single boon —

104

Give me one life wherein my days shall be
Blended with my Beloved's, till the whole
Shall count upon time's endless rosary,
A litany — one heart, one mind, one soul.

THE ETERNAL TRIANGLE

WAIT ere you kiss me . . . talk a little while —
A dumb, sad questioning lies in your mind;
Do not make habit your poor compromise.
Your thoughts fly like sea-birds before the wind,
And you are haunted by old oaths tonight,
By vows you swore so long — so long ago,
And hesitating, know not where the Real
Lies for you, nor just how you are to know
Your true allegiance. Hush, and I will say
The needful word; 'tis neither *here* nor *there.*
Old vows and new,— what are they but the flux
Of life's creative fire? That you spoke fair
To her, to me, and to lost women too —
What is it all, when measured by the pole
That with its far magnetic swings you round
And round the orbit of the Inner Soul?

We Three are One; we undivided face
With wisdom more or less the Great Unknown;
Allegiance unto One is unto All.
If Truth shall reap the fields that you have sown,
Let thy words die — old vows be less than air.
To lie with words, a fault; — but 'tis the sin
Beyond forgiveness when with issues we
Make falseness; with essentials and the thin
Keen edge of fair intentions; or when we deny,
Thinking to salve a lesser mind its pain,

Our own fair Truth, and so sink down to hell
And find at last our very souls have lain
Upon a bed of vipers.
                                        Do not speak —
Twilight burns on the hills; exorcise now
Those phantoms of old loves; death comes apace
And Spring no more will rim the barren bough.
Here swings the censer; here the incense burns;
Here the Eternal Athanor of Power,
Body supreme, transmuter of our dross —
The Rose Alchemical — the Magic Flower.

HOW SHALT THOU COME?

How shalt thou come to me? Why, as Love comes
In dreams that stir the sleeper's heart to burn
With phantoms of pure passion, undefiled,
That beckon on to dim enchanted lands
With murmur softer than the drowsy brook
Sings to the glade on summer afternoons.
Come with the sighs, the panting, quick-drawn breath;
Come with the rosy glamourings that lie
Close to the heart, when Love's swift feet draw near;
Come with the shadows of that fairer realm
Of mystery that hides in thy two eyes.

THE OUTCAST

I HAVE not read in martyr tales
Of woman crucified:
Always upon a martyr's cross a *man* has bled and died.
And yet I know that agony, for on Love's living cross
Each day my bleeding heart is hung; I know the pain,
the loss.
The "*thorns*" upon my brow — the days I live apart
from thee;
The "*nails*" that pierce — my hidden shame: I am
not wed to thee.
And oh, the "*wound*" that tears my side — I see thy
first-born run
To meet thy smile: oh worse than death, for *I* — I
have no son.

I CAN GIVE UP THY FAME

I CAN give up thy fame,
The wearing of thy name,
Everything dear to me,
Save bearing pain for thee.

I can — in ghostly tomb —
Lay unborn of my womb,
Yet must I while on earth
Keep travail-pain of birth.

Lest I die unfulfilled
(Star-dust the Master willed),—
Barren, I still must know
Birth's fiery, orphic woe

Till a diviner morn
Mine Own Self be fairly born,—
Child of the dreaded pain
That Love gav'st and gav'st again.

LOVE

I LISTENED all the night —
God did not speak a word;
I only heard my own wild heart,
With its wild longings stirred.

I looked to the farthest star;
God did not show His face;
Between the moon and me there shone
A phantom with your grace.

I felt the livelong night
God was not anywhere
In heaven or upon the earth,—
But you and I were there.

THE VOICE OF RALA

I HAVE never borne thee child, My Lord, in all the weary years
When I was thy slave in Rajiput, where they sold me, filled with fears;

I have not given the greatest gift, the fruit of our blended breath;
I have not cried with a mother's pain in the hush of the valley of death.

Thou hast kept me free in tenderness from blight that would me destroy;
Thou hast buried thy face upon my breast and made of me a toy.

As a woman should, I gave delight; I have known thy ecstasy;
I have worn thy gold and graced thy house, almost — have I been free.

Yet thou lovest me not; thou art lonely still, asleep upon my heart,
And I may not have and I may not hold — save as a thing apart.

This I pray thee, Lord, in thy mercy see, and grant me flesh of thy flesh —
Thy beauty shaped to a newer life and wrapped in a finer mesh;

For no decree of the deathless gods can sully the bliss
that's won
By the selfless loving a mother knows who gives her
life to a son!

And if breath of his life drinks mine, My Lord, still
shall I say, " 'Tis well!"
Gift for thy gift have I given, Lord, and there is no
more to tell.

He shall be strong as the Devas of Light, and wise as
the soul of the sea,
And out of Thy princeling's eyes, My Lord, the mother
shall look on Thee.

YESTERDAY

(Boston, 1910)

THE wind blew cold o'er the frozen fen,
And hurried back to the North again:
(And nowhere my Love did pass.)
It harried the icy fruit of the thorn
And the shivering birds that sat forlorn
In the barberries, hiding each downy head
Under their wings for lack of a bed,
(And my Love came not, alas!)

I climbed the arch of the ancient bridge,
Where the ice clung fast in a frozen ridge.
(And never my Love came nigh.)
And the icicles clattering fell below
On the frozen brook, and the quiet snow
Buried them deep to rest at last,
Safe from the whip of the northern blast.
(Oh, blue was his bonny eye.)

The late primrose and the windflower lay
But bare, brown stalks of the year's decay.
(Oh, how could my Love come here?)
My voice was dumb that had shrieked aloud,
And my heart lay wrapped in a wintry shroud;
So I hid it there in the frozen fen,
To sleep till the spring shall come again.
(For never my Love walks here.)

THE LAST GIFT

DEATH waits without; God takes me first, Beloved,
  While yet 'tis spring.
Ere summer's poppies are pale-scarlet budded
  My soul takes wing.

I have no speech to comfort thee, Beloved;
  I shall have said
Love's utmost word, and poured love's lavish giving
  Ere I am dead.

Yet in my hand one gift for thee, Beloved,—
  Love's last — and best:
You shall forget me in the golden summer
  When I'm at rest.

THE VISION

I LOOKED upon the face of Love one day
When you lay in my arms, your head upon my breast;
Across your face there swept a sudden change,
And lo, Love lay within my arms at rest.

You were forgotten, nay, had *never been,*
And only Love held thrall my soul and fate;
The world swirled into darkness; far away
I heard a wild dove calling to his mate.

So having seen Love, why, I love you not,
Nor any of the time; not knowing, I loved Love,
That one transcendent vision pays for all —
Peace! hark the cooing of yon nesting dove.

I HELD JOY IN MY HAND

I HELD Joy in my hand —
A wild bird from mountains Arcadian.
I heard his heart beat and the swift flutter of his wing;
Knew that he would fly, leaving me alone,
Once I unloosed the fingers that pressed close.
So Joy bode with me, captive, for a day;
Then hushed his heartbeats, ceased the flutter of his wing;
Afright, I oped my hand — there, never more to pipe
The sweet, wild carol of a far off land,
Lay dead the swift bird Joy, and all my song was mute.

THE BLUE ENAMEL WATCH

There lay the shimmering, blue, enameled disk,
Nestled in satin amber as the dawn.
Clutched to its heart the *immemorial years.*

I was affronted that this azure toy
Should be the mask of the devourer, Time;
Should be the servant of that gnawing tooth
That crumbled Nineveh and Thebes away,
And crushed the golden towers of Samarcand.

Tick-tock, tick-tock, this toy shall coldly count
The flying seconds of our fadeless joy;
Tick-tock, tick-tock, this plaything's chime shall toll
When Sorrow shakes her tears upon the hours;
Tick-tock, tick-tock, this pretty baud shall tell
When, like a sigh, my last breath floats away;
Tick-tock, tick-tock . . . the endless rune will run
When yesterday's oblivion holds thy years.

Yet will I love this marker of my times —
And love *thee* more, knowing its gilded dial
That murmurs, with faint chirruped choristy,
Only the lie that masks God's timeless heaven,
Where thou and I in joined ecstasy,
Without beginning, and without an end,
Circle the Dial of Eternity.

THE SECRET

I WOULD not bend to fate's decree
That gave a single life to me.
And ere my heart was cold and still,
By might of my celestial will
I drew another life to me
That fed my soul with ecstasy:
A secret life I could not share
With common earth and common air;
A love that would not be denied,
That all my being glorified.
I lived this life — to me so dear —
Without regret, without a fear,
And all my ardors offered up
To life within love's golden cup:
For love I must — (Oh, best and worst
Of being,— that *insatiate thirst*).

With soft caresses and with tears
I ringed the dial of the years;
But ah, cold, unfeeling world
Its anathemas at me hurled;
And then upon a bitter day
My idol crumbled unto clay,
And I was left to die alone
Shame's cruel death that doth atone
The body's sins. I sank below

A weight profound that, pressing slow,
Crushed out my life-blood drop by drop;
The blinding torture did not stop
Until cool clods of earth did rest
Upon the warmth of my still breast.
For Shame had killed my spirit's pride,
And at the last my body died.
Oh, gentle as a passing breath
Or as sweet sleep, the body's death
To me (who oft had died ere this);
I welcomed death's benignant kiss.
Long, long I lay in silence there,
Shut from the sweet and blowing air,
Shut from the roses and the rain,
Whose touch I might not know again;
Long, long I lay, till music stole
Within my dark and narrow hole;
There was such singing near my wall,
I could not hear the grave-worms crawl.

When I found strength to burst the sod,
My soul went singing up to God;
Rebellious still, it bade Him give
Me yet a thousand lives to live.
And so He sent me back again
To feel the sunshine and the rain,
And locked within my brain the key
To all life's baffling mystery:

Whoe'er dies most lives greatly, since
All death but serves in life's defense;
Fear not to die, for death will give
The Soul at last the right to live.

DISINCARNATE

I AM afraid tonight: — the shadows wind
Fearfully in the streets. I am half blind,
Moving midst phantoms as an empty shade
That in the light must slowly, slowly fade.
Life was a dream, and I — oh, what was this
Old Body-flame that leaped and burned with bliss?

MY IDOL

My idol hath feet of clay!
Yet what matters it?
His head is of carven ivory;
His helmet of precious stones —
Rubies, sapphires and milk pearls,
Wrought with cunning of device;
His body of pure gold;
White thighs of silver, knees of polished brass;
So what matters it
That my idol hath feet of clay?

A WAYSIDE FLOWER

Dear Love, I am a wayside flower,
With grace and fragrance for the passing hour:
A little, wanton flower that loves and lives,
And all itself to love so freely gives,—
A strange and wayward flower that droops and dies
When love that was its life takes wing and flies,
But bravely dying knows not pain
If only memory of its grace remain.

THE AWAKENING

I CANNOT serve thee more; my little hour
Draws to an end; there is not any power
Of eager youth in me to hold my sway
Within your heart; and vanished is the day
I dreamed I gave you strength to keep your place
Within your world. All that was mine of grace
And inspiration served as daily food.
With spirit-flame I fed your restless mood.
You never loved me; memory will pass,
And you'll forget the pleasant, flattering glass
That gave your image back, transcendent dyed
With love's deep meanings and with happy pride.

THE SOUL'S FAREWELL

"O my heart, my mother."—*Book of the Dead*

O LITTLE heart of mine, that ceased
Its reveille for life's glad feast—
O little heart, lie still—lie still;
Thou hast my soul to hell released.

Hush, little heart! In hell's dark street
I would not hear thine anguished beat,
Nor feel thy torture stir the hours
With anguish at my life's defeat.

Hush—and I'll whisper thee a word
That my ethereal sense hath heard
Dropped from those weary souls who drain
Hell's agony, by whirlwinds stirred.

There is no way so hard and steep,
Nor any grave so dark and deep,
Can keep us twain apart that time
When angels o'er my sorrows weep.

Then in immortal flesh I'll stand,
And tear away thy mouldering band,
And pluck thee to my breast again—
The gladdest heart in all the land.

The soul's strong horror is alone
Enough the flesh's sin to atone;
I am so glad that you could break,
And lie beneath the turf and stone.

I would the seeping graveyard rain
Could wake thee into life again,
And while in hell I burn thou couldst
In some red rose forget thy pain.

Hush — hush — I hear thee beating still
Within the tomb. Is it God's will
To pour thy blood a thousand years,
The cup of my repentance fill?

Heart, I pass to the Dim and Vast,
Into the yawning whirlwind's blast;
Farewell, O broken and spent heart —
I take my Paolo's hand at last.

RETROSPECT

Five years, Beloved, since you came to me.
It is an hour — and yet eternity.
I cannot measure time with careless bliss,
Nor bind eternity unto a kiss;
Yet swinging over time, in heavenly weather,
Float all the hours that we have spent together.
Five years ago you won me by some grace
God gave you, and the passion in your face;
Now I can say: I win you every day
From out the commonplace, the hopeless grey
Of life, and hold to high adventuring
Thy soul, else that the weary sense would fling —
Crazed by the tumult and the endless din —
The Holy Grail unto a deadly sin.

I have my pride: no Pharisee may say
I drew you down to life's forbidden way,
Or deem that twain with me walks covert shame.
I build my life to free you from all blame.
Lo, the cold world sets judgment on us all
By fruitage; root-soil matters not at all,
Save to ourselves; and e'en the humblest clod
Where our life-tendrils creep sings up to God,
As I do now for this day of Love's days;
And He looks down and hears me set Love's praise
So high that every sullen evil shade
Of terror warped in flesh begins to fade.

You are the mirror of my God to me;
Through you I see ofttimes His frailty,
But never yours. I guess you glimpse in me
His weakness, twisting shackles to be free,
But never mine. . . .
                                        Beloved, do you trust
These fragile urns of rainbow-tinted dust
That soon will blow on newer winds away,
Nought but fair miracles of shifting clay?
Or do you find that inner pleasance bright,
More subtle than the airy wings of light,
Wherein abides our spirits' ecstasy,
And all our hoped for immortality?

I need not share thy love; no one can break
The charmèd circle, nor thy offerings take.
I give thee all — and that thou canst not do;
Creation through thee takes its way anew,
And part of thee goes on into the race
That in our love hath neither hold nor place.
Yet my soul shatters wide earth's heavy bars
And scorns its cell to speed the morning stars;
And on a flight with Gabriel this morn
I laughed at all my days that were forlorn,
And listened, caught unto a swaying mote
Of radiant æther, to a silver note
That came up from the earth so far below.
I knew that note: it was the murmuring low

Of thy love-whisperings. Then I surely knew
I must not to high heaven vainly sue
To give thee home, and child, and fireside rest;
I must give love — God knoweth that is best.

FREEDOM

I HAVE wrung out of pain a temper of the mind
That will not prison you from the free kind
Of living that creative genius needs.
My love but feeds
The wells of kindness; you shall never sink
Again to cringing servitude's dark brink.
Life is a mystic shrine, or else a hell so deep
The best to hope for is unending sleep.
I find the shrine — body and soul of me
Must on life's altar burn eternally.

I give thee quiet, undisturbed hours,
And days of dull indifference, when life's powers
Gather resistance, even sluggish ease,—
That soft narcotic for the mind's disease.
And time for every one — love for them too;
I am not miserly, not even of you.
Last, I give folly — God is not so wise
He does not play the fool in Paradise.

THE STRONGER BOND

I HAVE given a great love — and in vain;
Heartburnings, sighs, fierce jealousies, raptures,
That can never come back to me again,—
Given as a river gives to the sea;
Spent as lavishly as Spring spends her blooms;
Distilled the rare essence that was of me
The purest and best.

I have given all —
And in vain. For this I understood not,
That to a man the greatest love will pall,
Or he can give it up, thinking 'tis best,
And suffer long martyrdom, and endure
Scorn, hatred, bickering, and all the rest
Of life's pricks, and drink of the turgid cup
Of disillusion; for the egoist
Within him never, never will give up
The joy in martyrdom — the Game of God —
The crucifixion for the ugly sins
Of others — the ascension from the clod
That spurns him.
If you would bind your lover,
Be thou to him a sinner, and let him
Suffer from you, for I cannot discover
A stronger bond. He will grow close to thee,
Sheltering thy sin. Furies cannot tear
Him out of the delectable, deep pit

Of sin's redemption. This the tragedy
Prometheus knew; there is no other one.
Not heartbreak, nor a sad satiety,
But that love cannot filch the heavenly fire;
Else that love cleaving to itself must die,
Ash of the altar flame of sin's desire.

THE PICTURE

My friend, where do our little child-souls go
When we grow up? . . . Now Sandro's picture here
When he was one year old shows plain to me
That they go somewhere; for it is quite clear
This laughing sprite is not the grave-eyed boy;
This magpie child, not that still sober youth
Who cons his Cæsar and goes out next year
To peer at knowledge and find his own truth.
Where has the wonder gone, the heavenly smile,
The delicate, mysterious air,
The wise angelic gaze, the eager love
That ran wide-armed, the brow so pure and fair?
Young manhood is so rare and fine a thing
Unspotted (well I know your father-pride);
But there is something nearer heaven here
In this old picture; and I turn aside
To shed a tear that you should ever lose
The child within the man.

Beloved:

THIS is thy March child's natal day;
Wild storm and wind
Turn the swift circle round the dial,
Give him the restless mind,
The heart for every trial,
The faith to kneel and pray.

Beloved:

All the fierce stars have mutely met
O'er him and me.
March souls — March courage gave us twain,
Blended our destiny,
Made small our care for gain,—
Our hearts with love inset.

Beloved:

All the blasts hurtling far, storm-driven,
March-born fear not.
They cast from Mars' own chariot wheel
Down to earth's grot
Souls forged like flaming steel —
Fearless, their souls are given.

Beloved:

As each man's heart, so is his love.
To the March-born
Love is a keen and cruel sword,
Sharp cleaving life's black scorn,—
Drawn for a beggar's hoard.
March-born love only love.

THE GOLDEN BIRD

How can I live? The Golden Bird has flown;
The cage is empty; wide the shattered door.
I have searched everywhere; my soul makes moan
Unto my heart —" He will return no more."

I have hung lures upon the rims of fragrant days,
And from rose-thickets watched the whole night long
For flutter of his wing down moon-struck ways,
And harked the echoes for his ardent song.

There is none like him — my rare Golden Bird;
I cannot find his name; it is not writ
On gilded parchment; men have never heard
Once on this earth the singing sound of it.

But all remember how that once they knew
Somewhere — far off — beyond the seven seas
A country where he dwelt. There skies were blue
And silver apples hung from all the trees.

And all remember, held by Youth's bright glow
He bode a captive for a year and day,
Then swiftly flew — where, where, they could not know,
But somewhere in the land of "Far-away."

Then glad with memory, full-flushed they burn
Upon the moment with immortal flame;
Yearning with glad desire, they swiftly turn,
And lo, they have forgot his heavenly name.

ROSAMOND

Heart-break and heart-break,
And weary wind o'er the sea,
And oh, the ghosts of all the things
Love never could give to me.

. . .

He promised me a flagon
Filled with a faery brew;
And he promised me Fame's bubble,
And the moon — when it was new.

He promised me a palfrey,
And many a silken gown,
And that he would take me with him
Unto the shining town.

He promised me enchantment,
And a slave to tire my hair;
He said the village folk should shout:
" There goes My Ladye Fair."

Heart-break and heart-break,
And weary wind o'er the sea,
And the long, long years I've waited
For the things love promised me.

The silver cup he gave me
Held many a tear and sigh,
The bubble burst to pieces;
The moon is in the sky.

I care not for the burgeons
Upon my silken gown;
He never took me with him
Unto the shining town.

I did not find enchantment,
For I was hid away
Within a secret bower he made;
My roses all were gray.

Another rode beside him
Within the cavalcade,
And every hoof-beat of her steed
Upon my heart was laid.

The folk, they bent before her
And sang "My Ladye Fair";
I saw the golden sun beat down
Upon her golden hair.

Heart-break and heart-break,
And weary wind o'er the sea,
And oh, the ghosts of all the things
Love never could do for me.

TO THE WOMAN WHO HATES ME

Oh, learn to love me for thine own soul's sake!
Make me thy litany, though heart shall break;
(For mine was broken, oh, so long ago;
Its fragments made a lamp that soft doth glow.)
If we could know each other's breasts at last,
Weep hard, and mingle all the bitter past
With our hot tears; then onward, hand in hand,
Each gently loving,— why, the very sand
Of Time would backward turn; we could regain
Our Eden, lost through bitterness and pain.

THE PROFANED WORD

"Thou art Danae in the shower of gold."
Ay, thou hadst said it — heaped the golden word
Upon the page until sense, grown o'erbold,
Caught at the glory that the mind had stirred.

Ay, thou hadst said it long and long ago,
Ere yet thy memory had returned to me,
And on strange altars blown the spark aglow,
Spilled all the jacinth cups I poured for thee.

And I could cry unto the mighty gods
For that sweet burning, ravaged, golden rime,
And shake with fury all the sullen clods,
And drive my love beyond the pace of time.

"Thou art Danae in the shower of gold."
O ravisher with words, in that wild hour
I knew thee not; my spirit leapt to hold
Celestial Zeus, his glory and his power.

V

SILHOUETTES

THE SILHOUETTE

In this silhouette of me
Is the self you always see —
Just the line of me, the shell,
Not the self that I know well.
Out upon the crowded street
Silhouettes we pass and meet —
Shadow-shapes, bloodless and cold,
Cut to fit an outline mold.
Sin and sorrow, vice and greed,
Runs the line, the visual screed.
Where's the Whole Man? There's the sign
Of a Master in the *line;*
There is deathless beauty set
Even in the silhouette;
Judge not by this mocking shade
That to nothingness must fade;
All this semblance that you see
Set within mortality,
But the shadow of the Whole —
But the darkness of my soul.

THE YELLOW ROSE

Sweet, saffron-tinted, sensuous bloom,
With waxen petals, languid with perfume,
Clotted with sunshine,— thine the beauty bold
That flaunted in seraglios of old.
What magic thine, what sorcery of flesh,
Within thy velvet petals' luring mesh?
Ah, now I penetrate thy fair disguise:
Thou art a wanton — and thy beauty, lies.
This gold — thy face; that orange, deepening there —
The scarf that trembled on thy bronzèd hair;
Those shadows — eyes wherein thy lure begun,
Eyes tawny like a leopard's in the sun.

Whence thy strange witchery? O cursed one!
Thou art the Rose of that lost Babylon;
There men swooned for thee at the Satrap's feast,—
With hunger for thee, Siren of the East.

THE PHARISEE'S WIFE SPEAKS

I KNOW nothing about your life,
Although you pretend to tell me a great deal.
I am as far from your real hopes and desires
As the farthest star in the planisphere
Of heaven.
And what you do tell me is a sop for peace,
Told with inflections of falsehood,
With perversions that do not deceive.
I am a present necessity to your good,
And you buy me with a price.
But at first I loved you, and believed
That when twain became one flesh
They also became one soul.
I have only one thing to do:
That is to *serve*.
You do not reject service;
Neither does God;
And the reason I never came close to God
Is the same reason that shuts me away from you:
He will not share with me
His life.

THE SERMON

Childhood

"Grace o' God," the preacher said,
And the words passed o'er my head,
Nodding in the sunshine there,
Caring little for the prayer,
Caring less for the great choir,
Lost in its supreme desire.
But my vacant idle eye
Scaled the loft, and soared on high
Where the oriel window shed
Lambent light far over head;
Where the purple and the blue,
Glazed in a transcendent hue,
Shot their shafts of mellow flare
Slowly through the ambient air;
Where the incense's curling grace
Passed athwart the window's face,
Mixing with the violet air,
Mixing with the golden flare,
Mixing with the blood-red dye,
Blood of Christ, set there on high.

Youth

"Grace o' God," the preacher said,
And I lifted up my head
Quickly to the preacher's face,
Eager for the boon of grace,

For I felt that there must be
More in life than I could see.
Hardly did I sense the blue
Of the oriel window's hue,
For my heart burned so within,
Mutely wondered, "What is sin?"
And the rushing tides of life
Tore me with ecstatic strife,
And I felt that Galahad
Kept the faith that made me glad.
He was pure in heart, and I
Would be pure as he, or die;
And the psalm I could not hear
For my heart-throbs strong and clear;
And the light I could not see
For the sun that burst in me.

Age

"Grace o' God," the preacher said,
And I lifted up my head,
Graying with the flight of years;
My eyes filled with unshed tears.
Nevermore the child who caught
"Grace" from where the sunbeams sought
Ingress through the leaded croft
Of the oriel window-loft;
Nevermore the youth who stood
Valiant in youth's hardihood.
Yet acutely I was 'ware

Of the gold and purple flare
Streaming down the great nave's length,
Glancing o'er the pillars' strength.
Age could humorously trace
Wrinkles in the preacher's face,
Note the jowls, the stiff, starched band,
And the quickness of his hand,
Yet no less be conscious he
Thundered forth divinity
To my neighbor man agape
Like a pompous pouter ape.
All of this within my eye
Flickered as the vibrant lie
Sense imposes on the brain;
Then my eyelids drooped again,
Drowsy with the long fatigue
Of the mind that has no need
But to rest in some lone glen
Untrod by the feet of men.
And the sermon drifted by
Like the wind's vague choiristy.
I had known the deepest deep;
Was the highest heaven so steep
That I might not climb without
Help of all this Sabbath rout?
Then the organ veered away
To the treble's flecksome play;
Solemnly above my head,
"Grace o' God," the preacher said.

Suddenly my soul took wing,
Far above the human thing
That sat dumbly with its kind,
Prisoner to the common mind;
And transcendent glory shed
" Grace o' God " upon my head.

THE GLEAM

WHAT is the joy within me
That I dream?
What the power, the nameless glory —
Where the Gleam?

Why this recollection tragic?
Memory
Of a sunlit, wide dominion
Curses me.

Life's cup passes me unheeded;
My lips burn;
For Olympian mead once tasted
Oft they yearn.

Was it God's imperial cunning
Me to bind
To the skies, lest I go loving
Mortal mind?

THE FREEDMAN

Oh, free me from myself —
Not from the Over-Soul, the spark divine,
But from this erring self that walks abroad
In all the ways of sense, and ever strives
Against the other for the mastery,
Turning self-seeking always to the end,
Searching for glory and the world's applause,
Using all kindness and sweet charity
To cover blackness so that men may say,
"How fair thy raiment, white must be thy soul."

Oh, free me from myself —
Burn out the dross, and strip from me away
The last thing that I love or that loves me
If needful,— so that I at last may stand
Loving for love's sake, purified and clean.

EGO

I PINE for empire. On this puny sphere,
What worth the tinseled panoply of man,—
His gilded trappings and his thrones of state?
Give me great Sirius, or Alcyone;
Give me the seven Pleiads, or a Sun
All-glorious, for my chariot in the vault
Of highest heaven.
Or with flaming power
Marshall together all the morning stars,
And courier with comets my ascent.
Swing me athwart the vasty bridge of space
And on supernal heights set empire wide
For my dominion — yet is not enough.

ALL — ALL I DEMAND

All — all I demand — not a part of life,
(Not the whining, lean ascetic's glass,
Nor the purple thick drink of the beast),
But the rich red wine of life — flowing and flowing —
All joy for my heart, yea, and all sorrow,—
The foam and the dregs — the bitter and sweet.
All I demand — a rounded completeness,
The wide world and its strange, strange byways;
Jewels of the East and steel of the West;
Heat of the tropics that beats on my forehead;
Cold that numbs to the bones' very marrow;
Pleasure that tilts on the fingers of Folly;
Joy that the blood in the veins surely speaks;
Grimness of life in the desolate fastnesses;
Grief and heartbreaking — remorse and regret.
All — all the gamut of living,
Up from the red of life to its ultimate violet,
Ascending, descending, rising at last —
Undertones, overtones, merging and blending,—
All — all I demand — the fullness of life.

NARADA

Before Time was,
When the Soul of Things
Moved on the earth
And made heavy the waters,
Came I, Narada,—
I, the Lode-stone,
I, the Man-force.
Out of ooze and steam,
From the slime of earth,
Slowly I 'gan to shape
That to be man.
Eons and eons
Great forms I moulded,
Finer each strand of life
Till the God unfolded.

THE BODY

I

Marvel and wonder of the tinted flesh,
What and whence are you that the world must guess
Always the meaning in your scented mesh?

II

What does the warm red creeping through
The ivory, the eyes' soft blue,
All of the blendings — hue upon hue —

III

Mean in the end? Just the chrysalis shell
For the soul that pure from God's fingers fell;
So we believe that His hand meant well.

IV

What one of us here (knowing his sins)
Shall say where soul ends and body begins,
Where the fibres are caught, where the fabric thins?

V

What one of us here (feeling color and line,
All that is subtle and sweet and fine
Of body of yours and of body of mine)

VI

Dare deny that this lives alway,—
Heaven's gold, but this tinted clay?
See — even God does not say me nay!

PAVLOWA

Thou who hast conquered mortal birth
And ceased to dwell upon the earth,
Save as a bird or fairy sprite,
With trippings on the moonbeams' light,
And twinklings in the evening sky
Like planets when the moon is high,—
Thou art the frond upon the wave,
The curling foam where sea nymphs lave,
And all the wanton winds that blow;
And all the fairest flowers that grow
Have bathed thee with their essence sweet,
And lent their grace unto thy feet;
And thou hast made me feel at last
The deathless passion of the past,
And through the dusk to see the face
Of the great ardor of thy race.

DEATH AT DAWN

Burn, candle flame,
Burn — burn —
In the night's turn
Till the grey new day
Sifts through the dark;
Then flicker and go out;
Leap in thy dying rout;
Let thy last lingering spark
Sink into darkness' urn,
And thy blue spiral stay
Not longer than the play
Of the fleeced clouds that drive
Where day begins to shrive
With white dawn the plumaged sky.

Die, candle flame,
Die — die —
Quick, spirit, quick, and fly
Ere the white dawn,
Like the still swan,
Move silently the night upon
Out to the sea
Of Eternity.

PEACOCK FEATHERS

(In ancient times there was a method of divining by means of gazing upon peacock feathers)

Peacock, peacock, peacock feather,
Only you can tell me whether
Fate will break or loose my tether.
Argus-eyed,
Old enchantment,—
If I sighed,
Moped and cried,
Laughed and lied,
Begged you once to drop an eyelid
Bronze and golden
Over azure beauty that's beholden,
Close that fateful orbit of ill omen,
Would you,— if I gave your stately mistress
For her preening neck a golden circlet?
Would you, if I gave her silver anklets
And one shining, silken, wavy love-tress?

THE SPHINX

CHEPHREN, he who reared the stone,
In the desert there alone,
Of the ancient pyramid
Where Rameses' bones lie hid,
Musing under Egypt's moon,
Heard the Nilus waters croon,
Whispering " Make incarnate now
On the desert's burning brow
What I bid thee, as thou can:
Carve the head of God-like man,
And the head must sink to rest
On a woman's rounded breast,—
Cruel paw and bestial soul
Round the riddle to a whole:
Man and woman linked to beast —
(Yet not all, these are the least).
Over the tremendous pile
That Time's hand may not defile
Spread the terror and the awe
Drawn from out the Ancient Law,—
Rear it grim and huge and dumb
For the endless years to come."

Now a hundred leagues of sand
Over Pharaoh's palace stand;
But men wag their tongues to tell
Whence the Sphinx, and what its spell;
They shall never set it free,
For the spell is "*Mystery.*"

GREAT SOULS

Great souls are like the pale sea shells that hold
Ever the music of the murmurous sea
That once their rosy-tinting did enfold:
They breathe to us of an infinity
Where purer love than our sad hearts have known
Fell wave on wave of radiance, beating free
Until the echo of its surge has flown
With them, that we may sense divinity.

THE STREET SINGER

He is some shepherd lad from Mytilene
Incarnate here, that the pure lyric art
Of cunning soft-blown reeds remain on earth.
One pipe he blows, one rhythm all his art;
That one so sweet that men forget to sow,
Or leave their harvests at the sound thereof —
A clear, soft note that snares the listening ear
With rarest melody. Seers sleep forgot,—
But he who pipes lives long in memory.

ARCADY

Oh, sing to me of Arcady —
My loved, my long lost Arcady!
Sing while I dream and, dreaming, float
A prisoner on Fancy's boat
Down the winding, winding river,
Where the water-lilies ever
Weave a toil of sweetness 'round me
To enchant me and confound me.

Sing, while I pass the gate that gleams,
Fair entrance to the land of dreams.
There to the sky rise milk-white towers;
There bloom the never-fading flowers;
(O eyes that never mine shall meet,
O lips that never mine shall greet;
Memory of your sweetness holds me;
Glamour of the past enfolds me).

Sing on, sing on of Arcady;
Sing, that my fleeting dream may stay
And waft me, wind of long ago
(O wind of all the winds that blow),
Down the winding, winding river,
Where the water-lilies ever
Weave a toil of sweetness 'round me
To enchant me and confound me.

THE BARRIER

THEY walk on either hand, two who are dead;
In Paradise they are not quieted
For sake of the sweet, mortal love they bore
You flesh to flesh, as they ne'er loved before.
I may not love you tho my heart doth break
And subtle pains my soul and body shake,
For white hands rise between your face and mine
And in your eyes I read a death-taught sign.
I may not claim your kiss; there lies a seal
That death has set, that life may not reveal.
For ever this wan barrier is set
Between our living lips that might have met.
Your way may not be mine; always I see
Those ghostly arms that draw you far from me.
So loving you, I pass with unshed tears
Alone, to dwell apart the weary years.
Lo, now they smile as they glide to and fro,—
Those two dead women whom you used to know!

HEARTACHE

THERE is a little sting within my heart
The live-long day;
A little ache wherein sense hath no part
To always stay.
And all the summer days are feverish grown;
There is no rest;
Nor in the cool, green grass is solace strown;
Only her breast
May soothe me,— that which I may never gain
For love of mine;
Never her touch may ease my heart its pain;
Nor word nor sign
Come as a boon to gladden my soul's night;
Only her face
Crosses the sun before my clouded sight,
With wistful grace.
I am so weary of the endless hurt,
So fain of peace,
That I would hunt Death down if I might dare,
And ask release.

MY BABY

Darling, I want my baby;
He is somewhere, dear, I know,
Wanting his mother to hush him
With rock-a-bys soft and low.

He's somewhere out in the æther,
A little, new soul unborn,
And I hear him crying, darling,
He's so tiny and forlorn.

He is one of the lonely legion
Of babies who never can come,
Who are lost and cry for their mothers
Till their poor little tongues are dumb.

And I reach out my hands in the darkness,
But, dearest, he isn't there,
Though sometimes just for a moment
I can feel his silky hair.

And sometimes he speaks in cooing
That only a mother knows,
And tells me his eyes are azure,
His mouth like a new-blown rose.

With hands and feet that are dimpled,
Perfect as flesh could be
That is shaped to love's perfection,
In the image of you and of me.

But perhaps we shall find him sometime;
So pray for him night and morn
That the angels will keep him and guard him,
Our own little babe unborn.

MEMORY

Thou who art, Old Memory,
Search thy scroll and answer me;
Search the chambers of my heart,
Where the pure emotions start;
Touch the curtains of my eyes,
Let old visions there arise;
Light this mortal mind so dark
With thy lantern's glowing spark,
And unfold to me the vast
Treasures of my living past.
Seek out all my restless race;
If I have forgot one face,
Brother, sister, lover, friend,
In the years that have no end,
Bring them here and let me say
That I love them all today;
For the bond doth never break
That is welded for love's sake.

TO CARA

SOMETIME you were a lily growing
Beside still waters — flowing — flowing
Down to the sea; and all thy happy dreams
God caught to scatter in thy tresses' gleams,
To golden-crown thee in thy mortal frame.
Still velvet-white thy throat: ('twere to His shame
To make thy beauty less); still thou must be
The chalice-cup of heaven's purity.
Dream on till God shall set thee, lips and eyes,
Once more a lily in His Paradise.

WHAT GOD MEANT

You cannot know how Art is given here,—
Not as folk think, from out some honey-jar
Of life, all gracious, velvet and serene.
Some wrest Art from the maw of dark despair,
And others mould their sorrow to a form
All glorious as a Seraph's in high heaven;
And so you must not rate men by their lives,
But by their visions, by that far soul-sight
Clad in the tinsel they alone can weave.
Why, I knew one who groveled in the dust,
Yet he could bring a star into a room
And coax suns from their orbits to illume
The art he followed. Who shall be the judge
What God meant for us, whether Art or Man?

VI

ORIFIEL

A DRAMATIC FRAGMENT

" But Adah sleepeth by the River Pison."
Charles Lamb.

" And it came to pass that the Sons of God loved the daughters of men."

CHARACTERS

ORIFIEL, an angel who has wedded ADAH, a mortal.
ADAH, a mortal.
ORA, the child of ORIFIEL and ADAH.
ZORA, sister to ADAH.
ZARIEL, a Seraph.
RAPHAEL, a Seraph.
AMIEL, a Seraph.
DEATH, a shape.
A host of angels.

ORIFIEL

A DRAMATIC FRAGMENT

Scene: *A glade near the River Pison.*
Time: *Twilight.*

[ADAH *and* ZORA *walk beside the river*]

ADAH

Two wings have grown so soft and delicate
Yet strong, a strange fear clutches at my heart —
His flesh scarce draws a shadow in the sun.

ZORA

Within these shades thou hast become distraught;
No mortal foot can tread the shaken air.

ADAH

That is my sorrow. [*Pointing*] Seest thou the blue
Of heaven's high arch? There hold your eyes.

ZORA

Lo, a star falls within a golden trail!

ADAH

A star — a star — and yet my Orifiel!
[*She addresses the approaching angel*]
Glorious spirit, that doth drip with light,
Godhead incarnate within radiant form,

I lift the tendrils of my soul to thee,
Beseech, implore, that thou wilt ne'er forsake
Thy Adah.

[*To* ZORA]

Lift up thine eyes, my sister;
(Give me thy courage lest joy smite me dead).
He glows a comet in the liquid skies,
Rolling in billows of celestial light,
The golden spray of his beatitude.
He comes, and all the air is finer drawn,
And glitters like the dust of morning's car.
I breathe not — heaven's glory is too near.

[*Orifiel descends upon the earth attended by three seraphs and a host of angels. The child* ORA *runs out from the glade to greet them.* ADAH *speaks to* ZORA.]

ADAH

Cover thy head, my Zora, lest the light
Of his bright presence blast thee like a flame.

[ZORA *withdraws within the shadow of the glade.*]

ORIFIEL

Greeting, my Adah. Look how our fair son
With all the Blessed Ones of Heaven doth play!
Alas, that mortal flesh hath found no wings,
Nor yet a way to shed its earthliness.

ADAH

My Orifiel, I must confess to thee
A fault,— all mortal in its selfishness —
Yet tender, born of such a desperate need
Thou still shall find some pity in thy breast
For my sad weakness. I have kept from thee
His birthright, in my mortal selfishness:
He is full-fledged, an angel as art thou.

[*The child runs to* ADAH. *She removes the white garments that swathe his body, revealing two wings of purest white that spread with a whispering sound upon the air.* ORIFIEL *addresses the heavens.*]

Thou Word Immaculate, Thou Word made flesh,
The earthly seed has given heavenly fruit.
This is thy perfect law: passion assoiled
From sin conceives immaculate the flesh
With flame of passion such as Thou didst know
When sprang the Nebulæ in golden rings
When Orion strode forth in majesty.

ADAH

I bore him —

ORIFIEL

Adah, beloved child of earth,
Incarnate beauty, mystic, wonderful,
Fashioned of yielding flesh,— in thy warm love

I more than angel grew, and as a god
Usurped divinity, dared to create
Purely a body — an o'ermastering bond
Twixt earth and heaven.

ADAH

He lay neath my heart;
He is my son; I pray thee, let me find
Some childish fault in his soft purity?
Must I miss all the guiding of his feet?
The mortal needs the mortal for its life.
Within thy shadow I should faint and die,—
Albeit my great love, if nought should feed
The aching senses burning in my veins
For my lips' thirst, only thy lips can quench.

ORIFIEL

I saw thee sleeping in the starlit night;
Saw and desired with man's untamed desire;
Came to thee first in dreams and reveries —
A phantom, lest love's glory should affright
Thy maiden-self with some too ardent gaze.
I sought thee here within the scented glade;
I called at dawn; I whispered low at eve,
"Adah," and "Adah," till the echoes grew
A coronal unto the wood and vale.
If fault there be, that fault is mine alone;
If sin there be, upon my head that sin.

But look, my Adah, God has shrived the flesh:
Thou hast conceived a spirit without fault.
[*The Three Seraphs approach the wedded pair.*]

ADAH

Greetings, bright messengers. What gladness falls
Upon this humble star that here ye pass?
[ORA *runs to the Seraphs and clasps the hand of* AMIEL.]

ORA

Greetings, my Raphael, Zariel, Amiel.
Now that my wings have grown, wilt thou this eve
Take me unto the moon, the pretty moon?

ADAH

Hush, thou dear babe; thy wings are soft and frail;
Stay thou with me and fly within the glade,
And gather early flowers to deck thy brow,
And ruddy berries from the mossy hills;
And when thy wings have grown as Amiel's,
Perchance God wills thy mother shall have wings.

RAPHAEL

Poor Adah! On the eternal wind-swept hills
Thou shalt have wings, else were He not supreme.

ADAH

[*Continuing*]
And we will find the stars behind the moon,

And gather in the path of milky light
The little stars to guide us through the dark.

ZARIEL

The hour draws near.

RAPHAEL

[*To* ADAH]
The shadows of the earth
Must never gather darkness in his eyes.

AMIEL

[*To* ADAH]
Pure spirit moulded in immortal flesh
Upon this changeful earth may not abide.

ZARIEL

[*To* ADAH]
Old worlds spin down to vapor in the void
And new worlds rise, but Law remains unchanged.

ADAH

[*In anguish*]
O cruel ones, is there within your breasts
No pity for a woman's bleeding heart?
Leave me not in this fearful solitude,
Torn from my child, my little weakling babe.
He will be lonely in the skies at even;
No lullaby to hush him fast asleep;

No kiss to fold his eyelids unto rest.
If he must go, let him return each morn,
And I will kneel and pray the livelong night
He will not stumble in among the stars.

ORIFIEL

Poor Adah! I have cursed thee with my love.
The sin was mine, but thine the punishment.
Think not I fail in love: such love I feel,
Were I God's universe, all love, I could no more.

ADAH

[*Wildly*]
Alone, alone! Oh, mockery of love!
Give me my child, else all thy love is false.

ORA

My mother, do not weep. Last night I dreamed
That thou and I were playing in the sky;
Now that my wings are grown, there is such pain
To walk, I pray thee let me learn to fly.

ADAH

Alone! alone!

ZARIEL

The appointed hour draws near.
Raphael and Amiel, this tender one
Bear close between thy wings, and if he fails,

Raise him unto the heavens, floating free
On thy strong pinions. I with Orifiel
Shall follow swift behind thee to the heights.

ORIFIEL

[*To* ADAH]
Adah, my Adah, hear me: let thy heart
Give back the blood unto each fainting vein.
I love thee, love thee,— am thy Orifiel
On earth, in heaven, in hell, or anywhere
Thou goest. Nought that lives can rend apart
My soul from thine, Beloved. Now, farewell.
(*He addresses the heavens.*)
O Perfect Love, above this mortal dross,
The pain, the toil, the weary sacrifice,
Uplift this spirit that is bound to earth;
Take thou our love and in Thy joy transmute
The earthly to the heavenly, that we may
Dwell as on earth, together, once again.

[ADAH *swoons. The Seraphs and the host of angels ascend, bearing* ORIFIEL *and the child with them. Darkness falls upon the earth; there is no light upon the river save that which streams from the celestial host.*]

[*A presence, a muffled shape, emerges from the shadows of the glade and pauses beside* ADAH. *She awakens from her swoon and silently interrogates him, half rising to her knees. The presence speaks.*]

SHAPE

I am that Nameless One whom men call Death;
Yet if that be my name, no man doth know,
For none that live have looked upon my face.

ADAH

Take thou my hand; upon the farther brink
Stanch all my wounds with thy forgetfulness;
The flesh dies hard; set thou my spirit free;
Unveil thy brow; love conquers even Death.

[*The* SHAPE *is suddenly bathed in ripplings of rainbow light. The mufflings fall away, revealing an angel of terrifying majesty crowned with amaranth; his wings, sweeping far above his head, are of living fire.*]

ADAH

And art thou Death? Methinks thy form doth wear
Life's semblance, so beclouded are my eyes.

[ADAH *dies. The darkness deepens. The angel of* DEATH *ascends to the heavenly vault, bearing in his arms the spirit of* ADAH. *Soon he is lost to view save as a point of light within the velvet darkness of the sky. There is no sound upon the earth but the murmur of the River Pison. The moon rises slowly and floods the glade with silver radiance. Where* ADAH *had lain beside the River Pison the moonlight discovers only a carpet of white, starry flowers wet with drops of glistening dew.]*

VII

THE EVE OF SANHAIN

THE EVE OF SANHAIN

Scene: A cottage interior in Ireland.

The father sits on a stool at the hearth. The mother is polishing copper bowls. ETAIN *is spinning. The mother speaks to* ETAIN.

MOTHER

Snarl not the thread, for no good husband waits
For maids who twist the thread upon the reel.
Now this way, cushla, all so fair and fine.

ETAIN

It is not I who snarls the shining wool;
A fairy teases me the whole day long.
I vexed her for I pulled a fairy herb
She set to catch the fat bees ere they fly,
And hold them captive while she steals their bags
Of honey, that the old elf-wives may sup.

MOTHER

There is a charm I know — a song sung thrice,
And paces marked and hands thrown up and down,—
To drive her hence, and we shall see this night
If she will go; but in the day, meanwhile,
See that thou keep thy hands from faery herbs,
And venture not upon the darkening moor

Between the day and night, for it is then
The faery folk have all their cruel power.

[ETAIN *stops spinning and comes and sits beside her mother*]

ETAIN

My mother, tell me, have none ever heard
Some word or tiding from our wilful Maeve,
Who wandered on the hills on Sanhain's eve,
And never more was seen by mortal folk?

MOTHER

Only the owl and titmouse know her bed;
She dwells beneath the little, singing hills
With faery folk. God's curse on them who weave
The magic veil around her blinded eyes,
That she must wander evermore, nor find
Her father's hearth, nor see that still we grieve.

FATHER

[*Looking out at window — speaks as if in a dream*]

Now all the hills are hung with shining webs
And banners from the ramparts of their towers;
And all our pleasant greens are ta'en by them
For revels, where no mortal sun looks down.

ETAIN

My mother, tell me. Cannot Maeve return
If she but wills it so? What binds her there?

Love is not there, for faeries may not love;
They have not souls to love as mortals do.

MOTHER

Who sups on faery food sinks 'yond recall,
Into the hollow of enchanted mounds.
Had she but closed her eyes upon their shapes,
Nor lifted to her lips their wine and mead,
And called upon the Rood, she might return.

ETAIN

Is there no hope?

FATHER

Yes, there is one; the sword —
My father's sword, the two-edged magic sword.
It was wrought long ago among the hills
And fashioned cunningly to sunder spells
And magic of the Sidhe. The hilt is wrought
Of whitest bronze, and inlaid with red gold;
His father's father gave it unto him.
It had come down from immemorial time,
Bequeathed by mighty folk from whence we sprung;
And never living man has clasped the hilt,
And never living man has drawn the blade.
The sword awaits its master. When he comes
A sound shall run along the burnished steel
Of battles in the distance murmuring,
The sound of chariots and armed men.

[*Knocking*]

FATHER

Enter. Who are ye?
[*Enter* CONOR *and* CONAL]

CONOR

We are sons of Finn,—
Conal, and Conor of the Mighty Hand.

FATHER

Greetings. Come sit ye by our hearth and sup.
Here is good ale brewed by Eleena's hand.
How came ye on the moor on Sanhain's night?
[*Offers ale*]

CONAL

Conor and Conal fear not faery spells.

FATHER

Yet you are white as hoar frost on the hills.
What sight has hurt your eyes? Here, drink again!

CONOR

[*Rises, sets down the ale-mug*]
My father and my mother,—nay, frown not;
I thought to call you once these tender names,
Ere my fair hopes had fallen in the dust.

FATHER

Thou wert my son, had our lost Maeve but willed
To choose thee, Conor of the Mighty Hand.
Alas she is no more —

CONAL

[*Stealing near the hearth*]
She lives, she breathes!
Start not with too much joy; the heart doth break
That holds not joy in custom's binding gyves.
Now hark ye; when I passed Aine's fearsome mound
(When all the torches and the folk were gone),
The faery court were dancing on the green,
And in their midst I spied a stately queen
In tunic of green silk with clasps of gold,
And purple mantle set with silver fringe.
Her plaited hair was wound about her brows,
Blue-black, as is the beetle's shiny wing;
Tender her eyes, and smooth and white her wrists.
Never on mortal soil walked one so fair,
Or worthier of love. And when we nearer drew,
It was as if some veil was lifted from our sight,
And we could know this faery queen was — Maeve.

CONOR

Safe and unharmed; yet whisperings we caught,
From out the circle of the faery folk,

That she is wooed by king of all the crew,
Midir the Proud; and ere midsummer come,
She shall be forced to wed this faery king.

MOTHER

She will not wed; some memory doth cling
Within her baffled brain, of other days;
They have not smitten from her mortal self
The blessed memory of human love.
Thou knowest not faery folk; they have not force
As we to bend the rod and smite the steel;
They work with magic essence of the mind,
With subtle forces and with cunning spells.
We who on earth have known the most of power,
Know it is magic stolen from the very gods,
Lost to all men, but kept by faery folk.
Why, thou and I could ride upon the wind
And calm the waves and turn the thunders back
Unto their fortress in the gloomy hills,
If we but knew the power that underlies
The simplest word. The singing sound of it,
Blown over blossomy meads, breaks open graves
(The dead but sleep, for death, too, is a spell).
Take courage; we shall win her back again.

FATHER

[*To Conor*]

Who draws the magic sword from yonder wall

May take her from their toils. Here, test thy brawn.
Draw forth the sword.

MOTHER

Hark to a woman's word:
Ere thou shalt test thy strength, look in thy heart.
No sword may win to thee a mortal soul
From the dark underworld. Look to the truth
Of thine own soul to win her from the shades.
The sword the symbol, in thy heart the power;
And many trials must be undergone,
And many dangers passed, ere she be won.

CONAL

Give me the sword.
[*Pulls at the hilt. It does not stir*]

FATHER

It is not thine to dare.
The magic sword sings in its master's hand.

CONOR

Now 'tis my turn.
[*Grasps hilt; draws the sword; music fills the air*]

MOTHER

Hark, there is music here.
Thou art the one foretold, the Master One,
And thine the sword and music of its blade.

Lightning Source UK Ltd.
Milton Keynes UK
UKHW021818080519
342334UK00009B/177/P

9 780343 593728